My Land

David J. Cord

My Land

Print ISBN 978-1-949267-56-3
ebook ISBN 978-1-949267-57-0

Other books by David J. Cord:

Dead Romans
The Decline and Fall of Nokia
Mohamed 2.0

STAIRWAY PRESS—APACHE JUNCTION

Cover photographs by Louis Handley
Cover Design by Guy D. Corp, www.GrafixCorp.com

STAIRWAY PRESS

www.StairwayPress.com
1000 West Apache Trail
Suite 126
Apache Junction, AZ 85120 USA

For Mirella

For Ninni

Book I—Ex Patria

1

I CHOSE ONE of those apartments where they find a months-old suicide after neighbours complain about an odd smell. The flat was old, dark and ridiculously tiny, suitable for students, drug addicts or divorced loners. I was the latter. I was a middle-aged man with no money, no prospects, no country and, as of a week ago, no wife.

It was in an old brick building close to the shoreline of Lauttasaari, a popular residential island in Helsinki, Finland. It was so small that it would probably be a human rights offence to house a prisoner here. The bathroom was similar in size to one you found on an airplane, and the kitchen had enough counterspace to hold a small laptop if you turned it sidewise. There was one window, which received no light that time of year—deep winter—because the sun didn't rise high enough to shine over the nearby buildings, even if there wasn't a perpetual cloud cover.

I slowly walked through the flat, carefully set aside the dustpan the previous occupant or his heirs had abandoned and stepped onto the frigid balcony. The trees in the courtyard were dead and bare and the ground was covered in the dirty slush which represented Finland much better than the bright white snowfields shown in advertisements. Reality is always different from what you imagined.

I had come to Finland from America with such high expectations. I would get a great job, become fluent in the Finnish language quickly, settle into the new culture, make lots of friends and live with my new wife happily ever after. The End.

None of that happened.

The electricity was off in the flat, but I could make out what I needed to see. I knew that I would rent it before I had even unlocked the door. Back in the tiny bathroom I stood on the tile floor and stared up at the ceiling. The shower rod was no more than a shadow. I reached up and grabbed it, slowly easing my weight off the floor. The rod held just fine, even when I jerked as hard as I could, like a body in convulsions. It might be quite a while before anyone noticed the smell.

2

My soon-to-be-ex-wife greeted me at the door of our flat with a notebook in her hand.

'Now that you found a new apartment we are going to divide everything,' Heljä said.

'Okay,' I said. 'Whatever you want.'

I didn't care. I had found a new place to live because it was necessary. It was impossible to stay with her any longer, but I didn't know what to do next. This question of who should have what was monumentally unimportant to me.

Heljä went through the flat, our flat, soon to be only hers, ticking items off the notebook as I followed. Bed, desks, chairs, couch, tables. I was detached, watching the scene from a distance. Do you want this, she asked. No, I answered, you take it. Item after item.

'Don't you want anything?' she eventually asked.

'I don't give a shit.'

'You never did.'

She then delegated what I would have. Two plates, two glasses, two knives, two spoons, this, this and this. A bare minimum of necessities and a few things she didn't want. She even opened up the refrigerator to glance at the food we had.

'What is that brown crap in the jar?' she asked.

'That is my rye bread root,' I said. 'I have been making Finnish rye bread with it for seven years.'

Heljä looked at me and closed the refrigerator door. I wasn't the only one struggling to stay upright in this new reality.

The sum total of my life turned out to be about a dozen boxes. She would keep everything else.

'Fine,' I said. 'That's fine.'

Heljä had a long-standing claim that I was always acting the martyr in our relationship, and my standard retort was that she was cruel and selfish. Both of us played our roles to the last. She was the stone-faced archer, and I was Saint Sebastian accepting each and every arrow.

3

Heljä posted an announcement of our split on social media, which is the way things are done nowadays. My phone wouldn't stop screaming notifications at me as the obligatory condolences rolled in. I had to take a shot of whisky every time I connected my phone to the Wi-Fi.

Among the waterfall of platitudes and sad emojis were a few offers to get together if I wanted to talk. I picked the first one I received.

'Yes, I want to talk,' I typed.

'Let's do it right now.'

I turned my phone off and put my coat on.

'Where are you going?' Heljä asked.

'Having coffee with someone.'

'Oh. Who?'

'Your step-brother.'

She said nothing but stared at me as I left.

4

Kaarle looked like a sailor and was one. He was short to duck under booms, skinny to slip through stays and shrouds and had strong, gnarled fingers he used to manhandle winches. He was in his early thirties and had some sort of fashionable swept haircut which my wife had wanted me to imitate for a while, before she lost interest. He and I had made a few half-hearted attempts at being friends over the years, but these were always overshadowed by Heljä. The last time I had talked to him had been six months ago, when he invited me to go out on his boat for the afternoon. I had to decline because Heljä's back was hurting again and she might want me for something.

We met at an Itäkeskus café to buy some coffee and those popular and hideous bagel-doughnut hybrids. I gave a brief background to this life event I was screaming through. He listened carefully, intently, and his face became grim as I spoke, like he had suspected something bad and was sadly resigned to the fact that he had been right.

'I don't want you to think she is a terrible person,' I said, perhaps lying.

'Of course I don't. She's my sister,' Kaarle said. 'But what are you going to do? Are you staying in Finland?'

'I've already found a place down in Lauttasaari,' I told him.

'Good,' he said, and after a pause: 'Do you need help moving?'

'I guess I do. I haven't even thought about it.'

'I'll get a truck.'

'It doesn't need to be a big truck,' I said. 'She is keeping almost everything.'

5

'This is hard for me, too,' Heljä said. 'I don't want to be here when you move away so I'm going to stay at Mom's for a few days.'

We went to a restaurant to have an absurd farewell meal together. Our Last Supper before the crucifixion. Father, if thou be willing, remove this cup from me; yet not my will but thine be done.

She offered to pay for her half of the meal and on the way home told me how sad and disappointed she was that I had accepted. I guiltily gave her a twenty in reparation but the disappointment didn't go away.

I wasn't thinking about paying for the meal. I was thinking about something else.

'There's something wrong with your soul,' I said to her.

Heljä took her overnight bag and went to the bus stop. I stood outside and watched the bus until it was out of sight. She didn't look back. I'm sure of it.

It would be years before I saw her again.

6

Kaarle and his wife Marjanna, better known as Mari, arrived in a truck Kaarle had liberated from his work and I went down to meet them. Mari had shocking red hair, a friendly face and the common Finnish ability to understand English but not to speak it.

Mari gave me a look which I had only seen once before, decades ago, from my boyhood friend Derrick at my father's funeral. It was a shy smile, an attempt to be friendly, clouded with compassion and sadness and a great deal of uneasiness. I knew exactly what was going through Mari's mind, just like I had known what my friend Derrick was thinking that long-ago day when I swallowed a downer and helped to carry my father out of his final Mass.

'I see you brought the boss to supervise,' I said to Kaarle.

She smiled uncertainly, exactly like Derrick had done.

We stood around in awkward silence for a moment, until I led them upstairs, propped open the door and grabbed a box. It was ridiculous, mentally the hardest and physically the easiest move in my life. The entirety of my worldly possessions was ensconced in the new flat in only a couple of hours, even including a stop at a gas station. Kaarle and Mari bought some coffee and I chose a Red Bull.

7

'Is your light out?'

'No, I haven't turned on the electricity yet. I might live by candlelight for a couple of days.'

Kaarle tried to smile.

'You're going to be cold.'

'I'm on district heating. It's warm in here now.'

He walked around the flat, looking it over and avoiding my eye.

'You should call Helsinki Energy.'

'I did, but I told them I would move in the first of the month. I wasn't expecting to move in a couple of days early.' He said nothing, so I continued. 'I like candlelight. Back in America sometimes we would get big thunderstorms—you don't get them in Finland very often—and the power would be out for a while. It was kind of fun to use candles.'

He nervously fumbled around, looking at the window, the stove, the bathroom.

'How are you going to cook anything, or use the internet, or even make coffee?'

I didn't understand what he was worried about. I honestly couldn't care less about electricity. Nothing mattered, including electricity. Slowly my mind cranked over and I realised what I was doing and what he was worried about. Electricity was necessary for life in the modern world. Having electricity should concern any person who intended to keep living in the modern world.

'I'll call them later today and see if they can turn it on now,' I said. 'I'm sure they can. They don't have to wire anything; just click a few buttons.'

He relaxed a bit, and the concerned look on Mari's face eased.

'Good,' Kaarle said. 'If you have time you should go see the

Lauttasaari sailboat harbour, but I guess you'll spend the weekend unpacking.'

'Unpacking won't take long. What are your plans for this weekend?'

'We're having a few people over and grilling some hamburgers and sausages.'

'Can I come?'

I blurted out my need without thinking. The thought of spending an unforeseeable future alone in a tiny, dark room was more than I could take. From the way he looked at me the same prophecy was going through his mind.

'Of course you can come,' Kaarle said.

'Wait,' I said. 'Will Heljä be there?'

'No, she won't.'

'Then I'd like to come.'

I thanked them out the door and went into the shadowy main room to stare out the window. Why was Kaarle helping me? He was Heljä's step-brother. He could have simply ended our friendship as so many others in her family were doing. Maybe it was pity. Probably it was pity.

8

The sea was covered with cracked slabs of ice like an old scab. A grey heavy cloud hung overhead like the hand of an avenging god and a few stray snowflakes drifted tiredly down. I followed the path along the shore past the bare birches and sickly pines. It took me out of the residential section of the island and into a semi-parkland, peppered with tiny summer cabins forsaken for the season.

I passed a few other people. Dog-walkers. Fanatic joggers in shoes with ice spikes. Old people with Nordic walking sticks. They were bundled in black and grey, dead colours of a dead season of a dead world. We glanced at each other's faces while we were some distance away, but averted our eyes before we were close in true

Finnish fashion. No smiles. No hellos.

The path angled slightly inward, away from the shore, so I abandoned it, ducking under low branches and avoiding emaciated bushes. The shore was covered in boulders and a narrow footpath in the rotting snow showed me where to walk without twisting an ankle. Birches, spruce and pine to my left, the vast grey plane of the decaying sea ice to my right. I brushed the snow off a boulder and sat, staring at the dirty white sea.

Little islands were scattered to the horizon. They were covered with gloomy black-green evergreens and dull brown rock. A few had docks. Faded red summer cabins glimpsed through skeleton branches. Saunas on the shore. People could go out there and live like a hermit within sight of one of the great cities of the Baltic. I wanted to be like Ernest Hemingway's Nick Adams and be alone and fish and cook my catch over birchwood fires and try to submerge the torment of my soul under the sound of water and the feel of a rod under my fingers. If I could even get there. Nick Adams had known the area he went to for his purgatory, but I knew nothing of this strange land.

I took off my tattered gloves and scrolled on my phone with numb figures. Robert would help. He would know what to do.

9

Robert is a pure Finn-Brit, born to a Finnish mother and British father. He grew up in Africa and the UK and moved to Finland as a teen. Millions of Finns speak both English and Finnish fluently, but Robert is one of those rare people who natively speak both languages. When he uses English sometimes you hear a South African accent, depending upon the word, and sometimes it sounds like he grew up in Central California. He speaks Finnish like a newsreader on the national broadcaster YLE, with a vague Helsinki accent, so I am told. I wouldn't know.

I had met Robert in an organisation for English speakers. Finland has groups for anything you can think of, including foreign languages. During our meetings Robert often talked about his outdoor activities, and whenever I heard him discussing tents or elk or mushrooms or aluminium boats I would listen intently.

I had spent hours out in the woods as a kid, exploring, playing, fishing or simply experiencing. I would lay on the ground on my back and watch the branches wave in the wind, or roll onto my stomach and study ants climbing up and down their mountains of dead leaves. My friends and I camped practically every weekend. To this day I still sleep best with a tree root in my back and an icy wind in my face.

It was a connection with the natural world which I had lacked since moving to Finland. During my marriage my environment had shrunken down to consist of my flat and neighbouring grocery stores. We had lived in cities and walked on asphalt. Heljä didn't like the forests with their abundance of spiders and lack of Wi-Fi. That big natural world which I had loved so much in America was gone, and I vicariously lived through Robert's tales of landing giant pike or trying to start a campfire in the rain.

'Robert,' I told him now over the phone. 'I have lived in Finland for ten years and I have never been mushrooming, berry picking or ice fishing. It's too early for berries and too late for mushrooms. Now I need to go ice fishing.'

He reacted as if I had told him I was having an urgent emergency, which I was. There was no consulting of calendars or vague plans to do it someday. That wasn't his style.

'That's your own fault you haven't done those things,' he said. 'The sea isn't completely frozen but the lakes are. Buy your fishing license online and I'll be at your place in two hours.'

10

'Are those boots waterproof?' were Robert's first words when I got into his car.

'Yeah, they're pretty good.'

He frowned. They didn't compare with his. He was decked

out like a professional wilderness guide. Tight-fitting and sturdy Nokia rubber boots, camo pants, thick windproof jacket, faded orange wool pipo hat like hunters wore. Their usefulness was confirmed by stains of dirt and fish guts and flecks of mushrooms. I tried to hide the holes worn in my jeans with my coat and fastened the seatbelt. After a moment of indecision he put the car into gear.

Robert and I drove into the country west of Helsinki. We followed the main highway for some time, before abandoning it for a two-lane road. When that had served its purpose we took a single-lane road. I had no idea where we were. There was more snow here, away from the sea. During the long drive he chattered constantly, alternating between stories of his wilderness adventures and his own divorce. Sometimes they merged together.

'It about killed me,' he said at one point, and I was unsure if he was referring to his story of camping in -30-degree weather or his tale of moving into his first post-divorce flat.

On a narrow snow-covered road Robert suddenly jerked the car into a tiny runoff. We climbed out into the cold air. In his trunk he had a handful of little ice fishing rods, plastic buckets, an ancient plastic ladle, a tacklebox and a gas-powered auger. They were scattered around his trunk haphazardly as if he had packed them in a rush.

I tried to pick up everything, struggling what to fit where. Robert had no patience for my juggling and slung the auger over his shoulder, grabbed one bucket and charged off. I packed the remainder into the other bucket, picked up the tacklebox, shut the trunk and followed him.

The Finnish forest isn't like the forest of southern Indiana where I grew up. Instead of maples, hickories, oaks and beeches, Finland had birches, Scots pines, Norway spruces and aspens. Indiana trees are fat and content with their long growing season while Finnish trees are tall and thin from their desperate leaps towards the sun during the short summers. The tree cover was more ragged than the complete coverage of a southern Indiana forest. The ground was different, too. Indiana soil is deep and rich from the accumulation of millennia of organic material while Finland's bedrock was only sparsely covered by thin earth. The soil of Finland was newborn, the area having been scraped clean by vast glaciers long after the rest of the world was emerging from the ice ages. The air was different as well. Finland smelled of moss and pine and water, free of the background pollution of America's Rust Belt.

I would have preferred to take a leisurely stroll and to experience the surroundings, but Robert moved as fast as if he were being stalked by wolves. I struggled through the snow, which came halfway to my knees. We climbed a small ridge and a wide plane of white came into view under the heavy, grey sky. A few small flags fluttered out on the surface of the lake.

'Are those fishing holes that they are trying to keep open?' I asked.

'They mark nets,' Robert said, and I saw that they were in pairs.

Robert half-jogged down the slope and I hurried to keep up.

'How do they stretch a net under the ice?' I called.

'It's a secret which we can only tell you when you are truly a Finn.'

My boots were three years old and had most of the tread worn away, but luckily the snow was old and had half-melted and refroze several times, so the surface of the lake wasn't slippery. Robert hurried towards a small bay on our left. It was about two hundred metres away and I soon stopped trying to keep up. I slowed down and looked out across the frozen lake. There were maybe half a dozen flags but no people. On my left was the rocky shore, thick with bare birches and bedraggled pines.

It was silent, grey and depressing under the eternal shroud of clouds. The clouds were more real than the earth. I felt as if I could touch the clouds but my hand would pass through the rotting birches. The trees, rocks, mud and ice were ghostly, insubstantial, faded, already melting away. The clouds were solid, heavy and titanic as they crouched over the world, watching and waiting for some event or sign beyond my imagining. The clouds of Finland were forever.

Robert stopped in the little bay and was stretching his arms when I caught up.

'Someone else has been here recently,' he said, gesturing towards a small circular indentation in the snow which I hadn't noticed.

'It looks like a good place.'

He turned the auger over, examining it. It was old and well-used.

'Ice jigger,' he said, still looking at the machine. 'You use an ice jigger to put a net under the ice. It's a board with a little lever on it. The board floats to the bottom of the ice and you pull a string which is attached to the springed lever. It grips the ice and pushes the board forward.'

'That's clever,' I said. 'But how do you make it hit your second hole?'

'You don't. You drill the second hole wherever the board ends up.'

'Oh,' I said.

The auger roared into life with one jerk of the string, making me cringe. Robert set the auger upright and began drilling into the ice. When it was low enough he leaned over, putting his weight on it. Suddenly it gave way and water gushed up. Now I knew why he was wearing rubber boots. He cut the engine and struggled to pull it out. About a meter away he drilled a second hole.

He gave me a small Rapala lure from the tacklebox and watched me tie it on the line.

'What kind of knot are you using?'

'Double square.'

'Hmm.'

I watched him push the line through the hoop on his lure,

twist the line around itself, pass it through one of the loops and pull it tight. It was done so perfectly he didn't need to cut off a millimetre of excess line. When I gave my knot a tug it came undone and I had to tie it again. Robert watched but said nothing.

We sat on the buckets and held the short poles over our respective holes. Robert jigged at regular intervals, so I did too.

'Cold yet?' he asked, eyeing my clothes.

'No. I used to get really cold during Finnish winters, but I think I'm getting used to them. I like the cold now.'

Unusual for a Finn, he only allowed a second or two of silence before talking again.

'What are you going to do? Are you staying in Finland?'

'Yes.'

'Why?'

I tried to laugh, but it was only an uncomfortable sound with no hint of humour in it.

'Everyone always asks why I came to Finland. No one asks why I'm still here.'

Robert waited, silent, because Finns know that silence is the most important part of a conversation. I listened to the crunch of snow under our shifting boots, but there was no answer there.

'I don't know,' I said. 'That's what I need to figure out.'

He looked intensely into my eyes, but suddenly turned his attention back to his rod. He pulled up a nice pike, struggling apathetically. He took off his red waterproof gloves to remove the hook and tossed the fish onto the snow. There it seemed to realise its fate and gave a few impressive flops before finally giving up. It opened and closed its mouth and stared at nothing, or maybe everything.

'Thank you, kiitos,' Robert said, folding his hands together and nodding towards the lake. 'I always thank the lake for what it gave me. An animal fulfilled its life's purpose to feed me and that deserves respect.'

I nodded. Robert was silent for a time, bobbing his lure and frowning.

'Do you ever pray?' he suddenly asked.

I turned from the black depths of my hole. He was looking at me again.

'No, not really.'

'I do,' he said. 'I think you should pray.'

Every other breath or so he raised and lowered his rod. I looked across the dirty white expanse under the grey clouds. The wind picked up in the distance and far away trees bent in the breeze. The wind came closer and closer, pushing through the forest, and finally hit us. I began to shiver.

11

I sat in the overstuffed chair in my dark, chilly and tiny flat and delved into my memory to see if I could remember how to pray. Even though I hadn't prayed in years the prayers came out perfectly preserved, branded into me during my Catholic upbringing.

Our Father, who art in heaven, hallowed be Thy name. Thy kingdom come, Thy will be done, on earth as it is in heaven. Give us this day our daily bread and forgive us our trespasses, as we forgive those who trespass against us, and deliver us from evil. Amen.

Even the old grace which my family always said before meals was there, complete with the chanting rhythm and lack of punctuation characteristic to how it was spoken.

Bless us O Lord and these Thy gifts which we are about to receive from Thy bounty through Christ our Lord Amen.

The last time I could remember praying was sometime in 2001 or 2002. I was a salesman for a financial services firm in America and the stock market was collapsing. No one was buying anything and I wasn't earning anything, so I prayed for sales, a very American thing to do. Desperation is fuel for prayer and Americans are a desperate people.

I got up, pulled my old Catholic bible from the bookshelf and sat down again. My mother had given it to me when I moved away. It was printed in 1957, and the title page announced Pope Leo XIII would grant me an indulgence of 300 days if I spent at least a quarter of an hour daily reading it. Yes, I'll take 300 days. I need it.

The musty old-book smell wafted up as I flipped through the pages. In the front was a glossy genealogy page to be filled in by the owner of the bible. Grandparents. Parents. Children. Dates for when we were born, married, received first communion, were confirmed, took holy orders, died. My genealogy page was blank. *I have sinned against my God, and have taken a foreign wife of the people of the land.*

The Old Testament God was a human god. He was like us, angry, prejudicial, spiteful. His human emotions poured out. The New Testament God was strange, remote, mysteriously acting through intermediaries. The Old Testament God demanded blood sacrifice. The New Testament God sacrificed His own Son. Sacrifice is the theme of religion.

In 1992 God demanded the sacrifice of my father through the intermediary of cancer. Somewhere behind the viscid clouds the sun completed its daily abandonment of Finland—it was 5:02pm—and I sat in the dark flat and remembered.

Dad had been excreting blood and our family doctor hesitatingly diagnosed haemorrhoids. When it became clear that it wasn't haemorrhoids more tests were done and the second diagnosis was advanced cancer. Dad came home and sat at the kitchen table with his sweaty forehead in his hands. He stopped smoking, which lasted two hours. He finally lit a cigarette with shaking hands and a look of distant terror on his face. It was too late.

My method of coping was not to cope. I removed myself from the situation as much as possible. I tried not to think about it, much less talk about it. I couldn't watch Dad die. I stayed at college and seldom came home, which brought a loud, profanity-laden rebuke from my older brother Wayne.

'I don't give a shit if you ever come to see me, but Dad is dying and you fucking act like you live ten thousand miles away,' Wayne said.

I had always been terrified of my big brother. He was tall, aggressive and eleven years older than me. Wayne was a figure of fear when I was twenty years old, just like he had been when I was ten. At his command I came home to see Dad, a bloated, unshaven and confused wreck who had to sit upright twenty-four hours a day because lying flat brought unbearable pain. He panted in agony and called out to his God.

For as long as I could remember Dad had prayed in Latin during Mass. He was distrustful of Vatican II, that 1960s ecumenical council which introduced church service in the vernacular. People in neighbouring pews glanced at him curiously, but Dad didn't care. He was alone, speaking to his God in the language of his youth, when the future consisted of limitless days full of hope. When Father Minta came to our house and gave Dad Viaticum, his final Eucharist as part of the Last Rites, I sat on the piano bench and watched Dad's lips move. He was still praying in Latin, but now his hope was placed on the next world. This one was dead.

His task completed, Father Minta said goodbye and left. Dad sat for a moment, looking down at the faded rug.

'I prayed so *hard*,' he said, his voice breaking at the end.

He hadn't been the only one.

I closed the bible and put it back on the shelf. No, I wasn't going to pray.

12

'Where's your wife Heljä?'

As I was still struggling to open my mouth Kaarle hurriedly said 'erronut', a Finnish word I had learned recently because I now had to check that box on relevant forms.

'Oh, I'm sorry,' the questioner said. 'No one tells me anything.'

'It's okay,' I said. 'I was kind of late finding out, too.'

No one laughed. Everyone looked uncomfortable.

There were about a dozen people at Kaarle and Mari's house. I recognised them all, but I wasn't entirely sure who they were and would embarrass myself if I had to say everyone's names. Some were Kaarle's friends and others were Mari's family: siblings and cousins with a healthy sprinkling of 'step-', 'half-', and 'in-law' qualifiers. Heljä had never explained these relationships to me and perhaps hadn't known either.

They greeted me as casually as they could manage and returned to their conversations. One person whose name I did know was Petteri, a relative of some sort in his late teens, sitting by himself on the couch. He knew English and was friendly, so I had often spoken to him during the rare occasions we had come to these gatherings. I sat down next to him and he pulled ear buds out of his ears, which I hadn't noticed before.

'Oh, sorry,' I said. 'What are you listening to?'

'The new Children of Bodom album.'

'I didn't know they had a new album out. I always liked them.'

Petteri brightened up and offered me one of his earbuds. We sat with heads together like two teens in love, sharing the sound of machine gun drums and symphonic guitars.

'What's your favourite song?' he asked.

My brain couldn't find any Children of Bodom songs in the archives, so decided to interpret his question differently.

'My all-time favourite song is *Over the hills and far away.*'

'Yeah, Nightwish is pretty cool,' Petteri said, as unaware of my Led Zeppelin meaning as I was that Nightwish had a song of the same name.

Kaarle walked inside from his tiny apartment yard, balancing a plate stacked high with grilled sausages.

'Are you guys hungry?' he asked in English for my benefit.

'Kylla,' I said.

'Kylla,' said a skinny blond twenty-something in-law with a big grin on his face. 'Kylla.'

Everyone laughed and Kari glanced at me before leading a line of people into the kitchen.

'What was that about?' I asked Petteri.

'You pronounced it wrong. It's kyll*ä*.'

Fucking Finnish umlauts. In the kitchen we did the ritual standing and waiting before Mari playfully snapped at us and everyone sat down at the table. Petteri hurriedly took a place at the corner, leaving me alone. Kaarle gestured at the only empty chair left for me, in the middle of one side. I already regretted having come and the strain of pretending to be cheerful was oppressive and tiring. I gulped a beer too quickly but didn't have the courage to ask for another. After a few aborted attempts at conversation I settled into an appearance of listening. Three different conversations in Finnish developed around me, one to my left, one to my right and one across the table. I was the dead zone where communication ceased.

I tried to be part of the group. I kept an interested look on my face, nodded when others nodded, laughed when others laughed. But it was a sham and they knew it. When the speaker met my eyes we became uncomfortable. He knew I didn't understand. He looked away and so did I, to turn my faux attention to another one of the conversations or to take a moment to eat a few bites.

It was acceptable to admire your host's décor, so I focused my attention on the walls. True to Kaarle's nautical obsession, all their decorations were about sailing. A painting of the Cutty Sark. A model of a 1920s racing yacht. A shadowbox of different knots: anchor bend, boom hitch, bowline, slipped sheet bend. How long can I stare at knots before polite interest turns into weird behaviour?

To my left Kaarle was telling a story in Finnish to the people at his end of the table. His voice rose in pitch and excitement as the story built and he yelled the climax to roars of laughter and pounding fists on the table. It must have been a great story. I abandoned my study of the incomprehensible knots and sought solace in the sausage on my plate. I had known Kaarle for years but he had never spoken to me like that. He sounded so free and happy. It was a voice of someone completely at ease, which never happened when we talked.

Kaarle was perfectly fluent in English, as far as that went, but he thought in Finnish. Whenever he spoke his tone and words were neutral, almost emotionless, filtered through the process of internal translation. He could tell or understand a joke in English—even complicated word-play—but it was subdued, a ghostly copy of the original.

Another problem was who I was. I was his stepsister's ex-husband, defined not by myself but by my relationship to her. This applied to everyone I had met in Finland, even if they did not know my ex-wife. Every Finn eventually asks: 'Why are you in Finland?' and when I answer 'Because I married a Finn' then that is how I am defined. I wasn't myself; I was some American who came to Finland because of a Finnish woman.

The more I thought about it the more I realised how common it was. I was defined by a dead relationship and a foreign tongue. This caused an invisible, semipermeable membrane between me and every Finn. It only allowed imperfect knowledge of each other and the imperfect transmission of feelings and ideas. This had been my life for ten years in Finland, but I was just realising it now.

Everyone eventually asked me why I came to Finland. No one—until Robert—asked me why I was still here. I didn't know myself, but I was going to find out.

I had been diligently working on my sausage as I thought, the buzz of incomprehensible voices continuing unabated around me. I looked up to find Kaarle studying me with an air of discovery on his face, as if he just noticed something and was trying to understand it. Caught staring, he had to say something, and he did:

'David is an outsider,' Kaarle announced.

The three separate conversations faded to a halt. Slowly all attention from the east, west and south sides of the table focused on me in the north, the place of darkness.

I said the only thing I could into that silence.

'Yes,' I said, 'but not for long.'

13

Jameson whisky was expensive, but it didn't make me gag like some of the cheap stuff. I carefully filled up a shot glass and got it down in two half gulps, divided by an involuntary shudder. The second shot was easier and went down whole. I looked at my watch. 7:19am.

I mentally gnawed on my failed marriage and failed life. I couldn't exist in a purgatory of thought, thinking of what was, what is, and what might have been. I had to act. I was a writer, and I had to write.

The angry glow of the computer screen challenged me so I sat down at my desk and confronted it. The thin band of blue at the top with dozens of buttons and symbols. Insert. Design. Layout. The huge white page, flanked by two bands of grey which only accentuated my failure.

I didn't have any freelance articles to write, so I had been working on my next book. Sometimes I wrote a sentence, or paragraph, or page. Rarely I had a burst of productivity and churned out chapters, great chunks of novels. Yet each time I read over what I wrote I deleted it in horror.

There is no such thing as writer's block to a professional writer. A professional writer writes, whether inspired or not. I had tried every trick I could think of as the days passed. I set goals for the number of words I would write per day. When that failed I set goals for scenes. It will take me two days to write this scene, I said. That didn't work so I set time goals. Every day I will write for four hours. I stared at the blank page, willing the timer on my phone to finally buzz, signalling the end of my daily torment and the beginning of my nightly regret.

'Aren't you supposed to write better after going through terrible trauma?' Heljä had asked me during the divorce.

Maybe for some people, but the experience wasn't making me a better writer. I couldn't write at all.

Wondering if it was time for lunch yet I glanced down to the lower right corner of my computer screen. 9:16.

If I couldn't write I would die. If I couldn't stop thinking about her I would die.

I rose from my desk, walked into the kitchen, drank a shot of whisky, went to the door and put on shoes, coat, hat and gloves; took off my gloves, went back into the kitchen, took another shot, put my gloves on again, and walked out the door.

The Finnish spring had arrived with its characteristic uncertainty. It snowed a bit, melted a bit, and snowed a bit more. The ground was covered by patches of old, grey, hard snow. The weak sun was trying to rise but was cloaked behind the impenetrable clouds, resulting in a sick corpse light falling over Lauttasaari. I tried to recall the last time I had seen blue sky but lost interest and walked on. It didn't matter. Nothing mattered.

I wandered down to the shoreline under the lights, half of which were burned out. Sometime recently a snowplough had hacked a deep gouge in a formerly beautiful beech tree growing too close to the path for its own good. The bark had been ripped away, leaving naked and vulnerable wood exposed. If the tree survived the raw wood would dry and darken. Over the years the bark would slowly cover it again, but the mark would remain forever. If it survived.

The sea was tired and grey, uneasily hibernating. I wondered how far out you could get. Coat or no coat? Would the coat get soaked and drag you down, or would it trap air and keep you afloat? A lady hurried past walking a poodle in a doggy jacket.

Neither acknowledged me. I stuck my hands in the pockets of my coat, gloves and all, and walked up the shore.

Nokia was a possibility. Everyone knew about my Nokia book, even though few had read it. I was still getting requests to talk at universities or various events, to explain what Nokia had done wrong and what the audience should do to avoid it. I could become a Nokia expert, being trotted out for a few quotes by the press every quarter when Nokia announced their earnings. Maybe I could write a sequel. The publishers were already talking about one. *Ten things every entrepreneur should avoid: lessons from Nokia.* Perhaps *Seven habits of highly ineffective people: what you can learn from the fall of Nokia.* Or maybe I could write something positive for once: *The phoenix: how Nokia rose from the ashes.* The company had failed with mobile phones but was adequate with networks. I could write about that. I could have a modest little career, a parasite scavenging the bits of skin shed off by the mighty company.

I remembered how she smelt. How she laughed. The feel of her soft, fine hair. Her wonder at stars.

No. This was all shit. There were other things I wanted to write about. I wouldn't be defined by one book. But why couldn't I write?

There was no wind early in the morning, so the only answer Finland gave me was the distant roar of cars on the Länsiväylä highway as people drove into the city. It sounded like a mindless monster hurrying along behind the treeline in an urgent quest with no goal. I needed another shot. Badly.

I hurried back to my dark flat and practically ran to the cupboard above the ancient microwave Heljä had let me take, because she had wanted a new one. I gulped from the bottle of whisky, took a breath, and gulped some more.

What was wrong with me? I had things I needed to write. Why couldn't I sit down and write them? I had done it before. I had written three books and hundreds of articles. Why was it so hard to do it again?

I took off my shoes and went back to the cupboard. This time I didn't stop until the bottle of whisky was empty. I hadn't chugged so much whisky at once since I was in my early twenties. I paced up and down the tiny main room. Five steps, turn. Five steps, turn.

Lying to others was one thing, but lying to myself was something else. I wasn't a writer. I was a fraud. I had nothing to say, and even if I tried no one would care. Even my wife hadn't given a shit about what I wrote. She had never read any of my books. I was nothing, a nobody. I was a fucking foreigner in a God-cursed hellscape of half-frozen mud.

A burp and a watering mouth told me the time of reckoning had come. I hurried into the bathroom and hung my head over the rim of the toilet bowl. I vomited noisily, my gags echoing in the miniscule tiled room. I puked until my stomach was empty, then dry heaved. I wiped the stringy strands from my lips and sat back on the floor and I spoke. I was more than speaking; I was howling.

'How could you, Heljä? Why did you do this to me? Why?'

14

The bathroom floor felt cool against my forehead. My head was burning but my body was cold so I jerked the towel off the hook and threw it over me, ignoring that it was still damp from my morning shower. Hangovers have always been bad, but when I entered my forties they became catastrophic. I felt so terrible that I couldn't even take advantage of the oblivion of passing out. My head hurt too much for unconsciousness. The only thing to do was to endure it until I could function. It took hours.

At irregular intervals I sweated and threw off the damp towel. Later I shivered violently. I forced myself to my knees to get a hair dryer and blow hot air on myself. I sat hunched on the floor and slowly moved the breeze up and down and around my body. The hot air released endorphins or maybe the buzz was soothing: I felt better, until it didn't work anymore. I turned off the hair dryer and left it dangling from its cord to lay down on the floor under the towel again. Vaguely I thought of the trope in movies and books where people in great pain groaned aloud. It wasn't a fiction cliché. I was doing it. I forced myself to be silent and time passed. I didn't sleep, but I stopped thinking, which was almost as good.

In the afternoon the mail slot banged and I heard a pile of letters hit the floor. I got up and gasped, holding my head. I faltered to the door like an arthritic hunchback and looked at the letters.

Stumbling back to my desk I put the letters on the stack of similar ones on my desk's keyboard drawer. It was only four months after the divorce and the stack was already about five centimetres high. I pushed the drawer in so I couldn't see them. Almost simultaneously my phone rang and I flinched, teeth gritted. I didn't recognise the number so didn't answer. I knew who it was and what they wanted.

My ex-wife had not worked and had liked to shop. Towards the end I had been too depressed to work. The end result of nine years of marriage was an enormous amount of consumer debt I could barely manage, much less actually pay off. Every month I paid the bare minimum on my credit cards and immediately withdrew whatever credit I had available.

I wasn't making anything either. I had written regularly for the English-language newspaper *Helsinki Times* for years. They had only paid about ten per cent of the market rate for writers, but at least they had paid. But now with their bankruptcy that long term source of income was gone. My earnings hovered around a thousand euros a month, consisting of a trickle of royalties and a few isolated freelance writing jobs I could pick up here and there. I was late on my rent, my pension, my phone, my electricity and a mountain of matrimony-era debt. In America they would have already turned off everything and evicted me, but apparently the Finnish law on destitute non-payers required more leniency.

I woke up my dormant computer and started googling. Isn't

Finland supposed to be a welfare state? There must be some sort of help available. Heljä had drawn on various programs for years, only briefly working a few months at a time. I discovered a housing benefit program which would help with rent. The information was in English and even my screaming head could understand it. According to the online calculator I earned so little money they would pay about half of my rent. I filled out the pdf and saved it to a USB stick. I couldn't afford printer ink so would need to go to the library and print it out.

But I needed much more help. I was rationing my nicotine gum and food, and the days of Jameson were going to turn into Koskenkorva if I drank at all. I hadn't bought clothes for so long that I did not own a pair of pants, underwear, socks or shoes which didn't have holes in them. I am a clean freak, and vacuum daily, but this put extra strain on my decade-old machine. The aged and brittle hose kept breaking and I repeatedly repaired it with duct tape. I couldn't afford vacuum cleaner bags, so emptied my one bag every time it was full. Surely the Social Insurance Institution Kela could help. That is what they were there for.

The Kela pages were simple to navigate and I easily set an appointment for the following day. Time to think about other things. Experience had taught me that my hangover would only lessen when I reached the point I could eat again, and I hesitantly thought I had reached that stage. Ramen noodles it is.

15

The instant the Kela lady opened her mouth I knew I had problems. Finnish bureaucrats speak perfect English if they want something from you, but if you want something from them they act like they have never heard such an outlandish language. She didn't even seem to know what a freelance writer was, but after explanations and negotiations we decided I was in the self-employed category. Apparently that wasn't good. I wasn't unemployed, so I couldn't register in that system. I did have some income so I didn't fall into another category which she couldn't or wouldn't translate. I had been in Finland too long to qualify for the special integration programs. I told her that I had applied for the housing assistance program which she hadn't mentioned and she shot me an angry look.

Now I understood why so many of the expats I knew were hustlers, constantly looking for temp jobs or little projects to make a few euros here and there. They helped build the gig economy. The old employer-employee relationship was slowly breaking down as the economy evolved, and this hit rootless foreigners first and hardest. They couldn't fit into the established system of employment and social support so relied upon hustling and their significant others. I wasn't good at hustling and no longer had a significant other.

She stared at her computer screen and I noticed that her eyes were not moving. She wasn't reading anything. She wasn't tapping keys or moving her mouse. She just sat there.

'If you can't do anything for someone in my situation I'll go,' I said impatiently.

'Yes,' she said in sudden relief, finally looking at me.

No byes or thank-yous.

I walked outside in the cold and rain and my phone rang. It was another number I didn't know. I was afraid of pushing buttons while they were calling in case I accidentally answered it, so I waited until they gave up before putting my phone on silent.

I couldn't remember how much money I had left on my bus card and I didn't have any cash. I couldn't bear the thought of standing at the front of the bus with not enough money for a ticket and having to get off, so I decided to walk home.

It took an hour and a half, but I didn't have anything else to do.

Two days later I was in a breadline.

16

I had the idea that I should arrive early to make sure I got something, but so did everyone else. It was an hour before the Hursti food bank in Kallio opened but the line of people stretched down the block. I got in line, with my hat on and hood up. Some of the people looked stereotypically homeless, wrapped in layers of filthy clothes, but most seemed better than I had expected. The man in front of me had on spotless, brand new Adidas shoes. I probably looked homeless myself. My shoes were literally falling apart. The sole on my right shoe flapped freely and sucked up any water I stepped in. My foot was wet and freezing because the Finnish winter had begun to regretfully lessen its hold and the ice and snow had begun to melt.

I was terrified that the press might be there, because they had run several stories on the breadlines in Helsinki, but they were nowhere in sight. Even neighbourhood locals paid us no attention.

There wasn't a lot of talking in the line. A few people laughed and joked, but most people were like me, silent and huddled and horrified at what had become of their lives. I heard a few words here and there in Finnish, Russian and what sounded like Romanian or something out of Eastern Europe. No Arabic, although I had wondered if there would be plenty of refugees here. The line was overwhelmingly men. In the still air hung a faint smell of stale beer and old Koskenkorva. No one was visibly drunk, but the stink rose from unwashed clothes and unwashed skin. I had done my part in contributing to the alcohol miasma overhanging us, but the shots I took before leaving home had no effect on me. I was too nervous and ashamed.

Someone I supposed to be a volunteer came down the line. She was younger, with a clipboard, asking something to random people in Finnish. She was friendly but had the no-nonsense and potentially violent demeanour of someone who works with unpredictable junkies. One man talked to her, but most of us ignored her. I shut my ears and looked down, hoping she would pass me by. She did.

How had I reached this point? I had always worked hard and understood finances, both corporate and personal. I was even a financial advisor for about ten years. I had written successful books. I had been interviewed by the Finnish national broadcaster YLE and the *New York Times*. All those dreams of youth. Perusing corporate reports, reading about famous businesspeople, dreaming of Manhattan penthouse apartments and holidays in Monaco. Now I was in a breadline. Such wasted potential. Such a wasted life.

The doors opened and the queue began to move. I shuffled forward. I didn't want to be here. I wanted to go home. But I was stuck in this line, carried forward to its inevitable conclusion. I was too frozen with fear and shame to step out of the queue and draw attention to myself.

I don't know what I expected, but I was surprised by the variety and quality of the food. There were fresh apples. Potatoes, carrots, swedes, onions. Canned vegetables. Rice, pasta, ground beef, milk. Baby food. Two-day old loaves of bread. Much of the food was straddling expiration dates, which was why it was here, but it was good and plentiful. The people inside were friendly but strict on how much you could take. You even had choices. Would I like this, or that? One of these?

I accepted one bag of food and hurried out. The line of people waiting to get in looked anxiously at me. When the food was gone they were out of luck, and there hadn't been a lot of food left when I was in there. I walked half way down the block and stopped. I looked in the sack and stared down the shiny wet street with the cold moist air blowing in my face. The sky was overcast and grey, the way it had been in Finland since the world was made. I turned around and walked back to the final person in the queue. It was an old man with longish grey hair, wearing faded black sweat pants. He anxiously cranked his head to the left and right to look down the line and jumped in surprise when I tapped him on the shoulder.

'Here,' I said, handing him the bag. 'You can have it.'

'Kiitos!' he called brightly as I walked away.

I went home and flipped on the light in the kitchen nook. I opened the refrigerator door wide and stepped back to get a good view of the contents. Inside were a half a jar of pickles, a bottle of ketchup and my sourdough root.

'That was stupid,' I said aloud. 'Now what am I going to eat?'

17

Summer had arrived. The brilliant sun had finally overpowered the clouds of winter, sending them back to the underworld to wait for their season once again. I posted pictures online of the beautiful landscape and seascape around Lauttasaari and raved about how wonderful it was. On social media I tagged myself at various places in Helsinki and southern Finland: museums, concerts, castles, the opera and literary events. Each time some organisation asked me to come talk about my book I carefully documented it so the faceless online watchers would know how much everyone was interested in me and my work. Every time I met a friend I posted about it and tagged them, so even their online friends would know how much fun we were having. Facebook, Instagram and Twitter received a carefully measured dose of jokes, self-congratulations and cheerful statements. I crafted an elaborate online portrayal of my life and maintained it for months. To any observer, casual or investigative, I was having the time of my life. It was all a lie.

The truth was that I was tired. So tired. Existentially tired. Existentially isolated. I was tired of being alone, of not being able to write, of not knowing what had happened to me, of not being able to pay my bills, of not knowing what I wanted my future to be.

It was June, six months after the divorce and the summer sun was shining brightly on Finland but not on me. No one called to see how I was doing anymore. Six months were an eternity and to them my divorce had been an event now relegated to the past. To me it was a process which was still very much going on.

My sister Ann in America was the only person who understood this. She was always empathetic and had a keen vision, and she suspected things were not as good as I claimed. Ann messaged me regularly and had an annoying habit of keeping close watch on my online activity. She followed or friended all of my social media contacts, even if she had never heard of them before. Sometimes they would question me about it.

'Is that your sister who sent me a friend request?' they asked. 'Do you know why?'

'She's worried about me,' I replied, which is a great way to kill a conversation.

I sat on a bench in the sun next to the shoreline in front of my apartment building. Many people were out enjoying the nice weather. I watched people taking selfies with the sea in the background. They smiled for the cameras. Behind them the blue green water was restless. How many bones that sea covered. Right there. Sighing, I took out my phone and checked in to a nice restaurant in Helsinki. 'Having dinner with my editor,' I wrote. 'Glad this is a business expense!'

Thirty seconds later my phone rang. It was Kaarle.

'Did you forget we were coming at six o'clock?' he asked.

'No,' I lied.

'Mari said you just posted from a restaurant downtown. We're about fifteen minutes from Lauttasaari.'

'I actually had lunch there and just got around to posting it now; I've been so busy,' I said. 'I'm at home now.'

'Oh, good. See you soon.'

I hurried back to my flat. Within a few minutes my buzzer rang, and I let Kaarle and Mari in.

'What's with the hair?' Kaarle asked.

'I was tired of looking like a banker so decided to let it grow,' I said. 'I want to look like a writer, like David Foster Wallace or Karl Ove Knausgård.'

Kaarle blinked. He wasn't a reader.

'I like the beard,' he said.

'Thanks. I always wanted one but your sister hated them.'

'Hmm,' he said and changed the subject. 'Hey, are you doing anything the first two weeks of July? We're going to take the boat out for our holiday. Would you like to watch our place and the dogs?'

'Sure. I love dogs.'

'Did you hear Heljä got a dog? She got it with her new boyfriend. Some little fluffy thing.'

New boyfriend. Dog. My mind turned that over a few times, analysing it. My ex was in a relationship and they have a dog. She wasn't moving on; she had moved on, while I was done and forgotten, still drinking and thinking about the sea. Kaarle looked at me expectantly, waiting for me to do the normal thing and reply.

'No, I didn't know that,' my mouth said, although I was far away. 'Is this the same guy she cheated on me with?'

Kaarle flinched.

'I don't know,' he said gently. 'I shouldn't have said anything.'

'Is he a foreigner?'

'Ei, hän on suomalainen,' Mari put in. 'Hän on pohjoisesta.'

'I found a love letter she wrote to one guy and it was in English, but there may have been several guys.'

Kaarle and Mari exchanged glances. Kaarle was saying something, but I didn't hear. I calmly got up, put on my shoes and went outside. I pulled my phone out of my pocket and for the first time in months looked at her Facebook page. There he was in her profile picture. He had a beard. I turned the phone off and put it in my pocket.

The sun was gone. I stared up into the dark green leaves crowned by clouds. A bird called from a nearby branch. A neighbourhood girl rode her bike down the sidewalk. Life goes on, so they say, but between the buildings across the road I could see the glint of light upon the sea. It was still there, still waiting.

I could feel Kaarle behind me, although he hadn't said a word. I heard the faint hiss of him taking a drag on a cigarette. He was doing what he was supposed to do: being there for his friend. What was I supposed to do?

'Of course I'll watch your place when you're on your boating holiday,' I said. 'But right now I'm going to sit in the dark alone.'

Kaarle shifted his weight a few times like he wanted to say something and then changed his mind. He gave the cigarette another drag, flicked it into a storm drain and retrieved Mari. They walked past me to their car and suddenly Kaarle stopped. He's coming back to me, I thought. He is going to say or do something to make it all better, but then I noticed his attention was on the sea between the buildings. He looked at a tiny white sail far off in the distance.

Returning inside, I took a bottle of whisky and sat in the one chair I owned. Time passed, because my computer powered off, the whisky diminished and it eventually became darker. Dark? I wondered. How long have I been sitting here? It must be really late. Today is the summer solstice. Juhannus is this coming weekend, another Finnish holiday I would spend alone. I should do something.

A part of my mind meant that it was late and I should go to bed, but another part was thinking of something entirely different. Do something. Yes, it was time. I had drunk and moped and lied for long enough. Time to either live or not to live.

So: make the choice.

But I couldn't. I had been living as an undead for so long I couldn't choose between life or death. I'm such a coward, always ignoring my problems. I ignored my collapsing marriage because I couldn't deal with it. I ignored my dying father, my catastrophic finances, my unwritten book, all because I couldn't face them.

Fine. I'll seek guidance. I'll do what Robert told me to do.

I kicked the chair out of the way and threw myself on my knees on the cracked faux-wood linoleum floor. I made the sign of the cross. I didn't feel like a hypocrite. I felt desperate.

'God, I can't do this anymore. Help me. Please help me.'

I listened but God has no tongue.

Cleromancy, I thought. Let God reveal His will that way. I climbed back to my feet and dug into the depths of my desk drawer. I had to use an American coin, so I pulled out a quarter. Heads I would give up my head to the fish of the Baltic. No notes, no call, nothing. I would just close the door behind me and go for a swim. I knew exactly where and how I would do it, too. I've known it for a long time. Tails I would return from the dead. Lazarus did not have a choice. He rose from the grave because the Son of God willed it. I would rise too, if He revealed His will by the flip of the coin. I would write. I would fix my finances. I would have relationships. I would live again. I would not be alone. One way or the other. End it or begin it. There were no other options. I couldn't live like this anymore.

I took a final shot of whisky and threw the bottle across the room, spraying golden liquid, and flipped the quarter. In that instant as it spun in the air I knew. I caught it in my right hand and laid it down on my left, took a deep breath, and uncovered it. There it was. There was my answer. There was the solution to all of my problems.

'Fuck you,' I said and dropped the coin back in my drawer.

Book II—Blind Dogs of the Sun

1

THE FIRST ACT of my *damnatio memoriae* was breaking off a birch branch about thirty centimetres long and slightly smaller in diameter than my little finger. I carried it in my hand and walked to the Lauttasaari drawbridge. On the south side, approximately in the centre, I plucked off the wedding and engagement rings from my finger and put them on the branch. I used it as an atlatl and threw the rings as far as I could into the sea.

Back at my flat I turned on my computer and methodically erased every trace of my ex-wife. Photos, letters, documents. Things I had scanned for her. Things I had printed out for her mother. Old emails. Heljä and I had met online and our relationship had developed by online chats. I had saved huge files of them, hours and hours of getting to know each other by keyboard. She used to sign off our chats with 'huggee', a portmanteau of 'huge' and 'hug', coupled with the diminutive -ee sound to make it cute. It was no longer cute. It was sickening, and it was all obliterated.

In my closet were boxes of things. Cards, love letters, photos, trinkets. They were euthanized without mercy. I not only threw away photos of her; I even threw away photos she had taken.

I had done such a thorough job that almost all traces of her were gone, but something from her appeared unexpectedly. As I was organising my books a little note fluttered out of *A visit from the goon squad.* I picked it up, at first thinking it was a makeshift bookmark.

'Have fun on your trip! I hope you are thinking of me the way I am thinking of you! I love you!'

I shrank away from it in revulsion. I must have taken that book on a trip and Heljä had stuck that note inside for me to find. I shoved the note back inside the book and hurried to the kitchen where I threw it away.

Looking at the cover, with its famous guitar headstock and tuning pegs, I felt a twinge of remorse. Jennifer Egan doesn't deserve this. I picked up the book, brushed off the coffee grounds and half-dried piece of nicotine gum from its back, and pulled out the note. The book was placed back on the shelf, but the note went into the toilet. I pissed on it, grimly, stoically. I flushed and thoroughly washed my hands. I went back to ordering my books but my hands still felt dirty, so I washed them again.

By the time I was done practically every memory of my previous life in Finland was gone. There was nothing left. With that cancer ruthlessly cut out of my life I was ready to go housesit for Kaarle and Mari. More importantly, I was ready to start living again.

2

Kaarle was outside waiting for me and smoking a cigarette when I arrived.

'You didn't bring much for two weeks,' he said, looking at my carryon suitcase.

'I don't have much.'

Silence. He finished his cigarette and opened the door for me. It was like stepping into a whirlwind. People hurried back and forth, carrying things, yelling at each other across rooms. I made my way through the piles of luggage and bags, dodging people and trying to find a place to stay out of the way.

Kaarle and his wife had a blended family. From a previously relationship Mari had eleven-year-old Minttu. Together Kaarle and Mari had two more children, nine-year-old Nea and seven-year-old Niilo. Niilo was my and my ex-wife's godson. We had met him maybe three times.

I edged my way through the commotion and moved a few bags on the couch so I had a place to sit down. The kids came in to give me a brief inspection and disappeared. The others ignored me, so I occupied myself with the frantically excited puppies. Mari bred Landseers, those giant, friendly and slobbery black-and-white Newfoundlanders. They had gotten a male and female, Santeri and Freyja, to make even more friendly and slobbery Landseers. But the puppies were more interested in all the excitement than some guy sitting on the couch, so they bounded away.

Out of my suitcase I retrieved a mid-sized hard-backed notebook. I had developed a liking for them from my journalism days, because they were perfect for standing and writing as you interviewed someone. They were great for writing on your knee, too, which was what I did now.

I. Money

II. Creation

III. Finland

Here they were: my three huge problems. I had to get my financial situation under control. I had to start writing again. Finally, I had to understand my place in this weird, cold country.

There was a tap on my arm. I looked up. Little blond Nea stood in front of me, smiling. She tapped me again. I tapped her in return and she ran away. Back to the notebook.

'You can sleep anywhere you like,' Kaarle said.

'Okay,' I said.

'Mari put new sheets on our bed if you want to sleep there.'

'Okay.'

Mari called him from the kitchen and Kaarle was gone again. Back to the three huge issues in my life. Back to thinking.

Tap. Nea stood before me, arms out like she was crucified, with a hopeful grin on her face. Lacking any better idea, I reached out and tickled her. She giggled and held her hands out again expectantly. I stared at her, at a loss, and she gave a slight hop.

'You want me to pick you up?'

She continued smiling, with no idea what I was saying. This was how I acted when people spoke Finnish to me.

I placed the notebook down, stood up and picked up Nea, her giggling the entire time. Nea squirmed around so she was hanging upside down. Okay, I can do this. Our game was simple. I tossed her in the air, caught her, and then hung her upside down until my arms got tired. She gave me a three second rest and came grinning at me, arms out like a happy Jesus on the cross, to begin again.

Niilo came to see what the commotion was all about, noted the game and disappeared. Minttu also arrived. She was distressed, frowning at Nea and looking apologetically at me, like her little sister shouldn't be bothering me. I smiled at her, trying to let her know that Nea was no trouble.

Mari walked by holding a big water jug and stopped. She observed the scene of me dangling her daughter upside down. Mari looked right into my eyes. She wasn't trying to communicate; she was thinking. What do you want from me, I thought, but at that moment Mari smiled and said something to Nea. Nea laughed and replied, her voice strained from being held upside down. Mari went on her way, her left arm held straight out to counterbalance the giant water jug.

Nea was tireless, but I wasn't, so I pretended I needed to go to the bathroom just so I could rest my aching arms. But when I came out of the bathroom she was waiting, arms out, with a huge smile on her face.

'Oh, by the way,' Kaarle said as he walked past. 'Minttu will come back a couple of days early with an older cousin. They will stay here a night before going on to Mari's parents' cabin.'

'They are? Do I need to do anything?'

'Don't let them out of your sight,' Kaarle laughed. 'They might burn the place down.'

'Sure.' An irrational twinge of anger went through me and I set Nea down. I didn't want people around, particularly kids I didn't know. I wanted to be alone and plan how I was going to start living again.

Kaarle and Mari made several trips to the van, carrying things. I tried to volunteer to help but Nea demanded my attention. Niilo shoved her out of the way and wanted to be thrown in the air too, but after one toss he decided the game wasn't for him and disappeared again.

Finally Kaarle and Mari herded the kids out the door, said bye, and blessed silence fell. A forgotten glove lay on the floor. A roll of paper towels. Shoes. Two sleeping puppies, their red tongues dangling out of the sides of their mouths, their sides rapidly rising and falling, worn out by all the activity. It was like surveying a battlefield after an army had routed. That was apt. In the quiet of a battle's aftermath was when the real work was done.

3

I spent my time walking the puppies, thinking and making notes. I was determined to get my life back on track, but I didn't know how to do it. I needed a plan, to know what to do. After hours of torture and scribbling ideas I wandered over to the couch and turned on the PlayStation. There is nothing like videogames to eat time. You forget about your failed life when immersed in videogames. So the days passed: thinking, writing, avoiding.

One day I was walking the dogs and I stumbled on a root. My left knee felt numb, weak. As I was experimentally flexing it a young girl suddenly appeared, diving into the puppies. Minttu and her cousin were back. After they said hello to the puppies (ignoring me) they went into the flat and I continued my limping walk with the dogs. I'm getting old, I thought. When I returned the cousin had already retreated up to a bedroom to play video games. Minttu had turned off my game of Assassin's Creed and was playing something else.

What the hell? She had just strolled in and turned off my game like she owned the place. After a couple of deep breaths I calmed myself. She did own the place. This was her home, her PlayStation, her TV. Minttu had every right to play her game if she wanted to. Besides, she's a kid.

Holy shit, I thought. Yes, she's a child. Standing there looking at the back of her head, I had no idea what I was supposed to do. I had no experience with kids. I was the youngest of three childless siblings and never had any exposure to children. Neither had I received any directions from Kaarle. He had said not to let them out of my sight, but he was laughing when he said it. The cousin looked to be about sixteen, able to take care of himself. He had closed his door, giving the unmistakable sign of a teenager desiring solitude. But Minttu was here on the couch. Do I ignore her and let her do her thing? She was so young, only eleven years old. Do kids that age need supervision? I honestly didn't know.

I sat down next to her on the couch.

'What are you playing?' I spoke in that loud, slow, precise way you do when you speak to someone who doesn't know your language well.

'Minecraft.'

She concentrated on the screen, brushing her waist-length brown hair out of her face. Her character wandered over the virtual landscape, digging holes in rock hills. The scene was purposefully primitive, with everything made of huge blocks like an old 8-bit video game. Yet it was a bright, cheery place. The sun was shining, the grass was green and the trees and mountains and streams were beautiful in an odd way.

'Why are you destroying everything?'

'I'm getting things.'

I leaned forward on the couch to watch. She chopped up trees and collected the resulting wood. She dug into hills and stored the rock. Eventually some unknown threshold was passed and Minttu was satisfied with what she had gathered. She found a nice open glade in a forest and plopped down a stone foundation and built it up with wooden blocks. In no time the footprint of a building emerged.

'You're building a house,' I said.

'Monsters come at night.'

I looked at her and back at the game. The cheery game maybe wasn't as cheery as I had thought.

'What do you do when monsters come? Do you hide or fight them?'

Minttu jumped up, went to the entertainment centre and brought back a second controller for me. She restarted the game in two-player mode and explained haltingly what to do. Soon we were traipsing over the landscape together, talking and laughing and building a big tree house so we could hide from night monsters.

4

Later in the afternoon I began to get hungry. Kaarle and Mari had left nothing to eat in their flat, and I had been simply buying food as I needed it. But now I had two kids with me. I assumed I needed to feed them. Adults did that, I knew.

'Are you hungry?' I asked Minttu as we played.

'I'm starving!' she announced theatrically.

'I don't have much food here. Do you want to go to the store? We can grill hamburgers.'

We walked to the store together in the bright summer sunshine, talking the entire way. I showed her where I walked the puppies. She pointed out different sights in the neighbourhood, like where her friends and grandparents lived.

'Elias and I go there tomorrow,' Minttu told me, pointing to her grandparents' flat as we walked by. 'We will go to their cabin.'

I blinked at her until I realised Elias must be the cousin. No one had bothered to tell me his name, and I had been too embarrassed to ask.

'Why didn't you go there instead of coming home?'

That seemed the logical thing to do, so I wasn't sure why Elias and Minttu had come home in the first place. Minttu looked away, screwing up her face as she thought.

'I don't know the words!'

'It's okay. It doesn't matter; I was just curious.'

That was the way with speaking with Finns. They could give the necessary information—Elias and Minttu are coming home and they will leave the next day—but the reasoning behind it was lost to me. That was all supplementary information, unnecessary to my job of watching the puppies and the flat, so it was never explained. Foreigners who couldn't speak the language were only given information on a need-to-know basis.

The store's automatic doors opened to let us in and we were enveloped with cool airconditioned air. At each purchase I asked her opinion on what we should get.

'Ten per cent fat on the minced meat?' I asked her. 'Beef-pork mix?'

'Beef with ten per cent fat,' she announced decisively.

I gathered minced meat, frozen French fries, buns and ketchup in a plastic basket with Minttu at my side. After we got everything I could think of for our meal I looked in my wallet and looked at her.

'If there is anything else you want, go grab it,' I told her.

'What?' She looked blankly at me.

'Would you like anything else to eat for dinner? Something to drink? Go get anything you want.'

'Anything?'

'Well, within reason,' I laughed.

She looked at me a moment longer, unsure, then a big smile

broke across her face and she ran down the aisle. In a household of five people they likely had a rigid meal structure planned in advance. I wondered if Minttu had ever been let loose in a grocery store before and told to get whatever meal she wanted.

She came back with a head of lettuce, a cucumber and a paprika.

'We can have salad,' she announced happily.

'Salad? You can get anything you want and you choose salad?'

Her smile disappeared. The briefest glimpse of sadness and apprehension flickered across her face before it became stoic, like she had done something wrong and was ready to accept her punishment. I felt a strange twinge in my chest.

'No, no, I'm just teasing you. I like salad,' I hurriedly reassured her. 'I also like ice cream. We should have ice cream for dessert on a hot day like this.'

We picked out a container of ice cream, but she hesitated at the freezer.

'Let's get some cones and eat them on the walk home!' she said gleefully, as if she had just proposed the naughtiest thing she could imagine.

'That's a great idea!'

'I buy this ice cream.'

She pulled out a small handful of fifty- and twenty-euro cent coins from her pocket.

'I can buy it,' I said.

'No, I buy.'

She went through the checkout line first to buy her ice cream and bagged our other items as they came down the conveyor belt. Outside on the hot tarmac we unwrapped our ice cream cones and threw the paper away. We had to eat quickly because they were already melting.

I watched her as we walked and wondered why she had insisted on buying her ice cream for the walk home.

Maybe she had been taught that if she wanted something

extra, like candy or a treat, she had to buy it herself. It was probably a way to teach her about money. I had offered to pay for it but she had refused, sticking to what she had been taught was the right thing to do. Her parents would never have known but she had done it anyway. I ate my ice cream in big bites but Minttu licked hers, frantically turning it to get the melting ice cream running down the sides of the cone. I laughed, which got her laughing, too.

You're a good kid, I thought.

Back at the apartment I shoved the fries in the oven and limped outside to grill the hamburgers. How could such a little stumble cause such damage to my knee?

I needed to write a fourth issue to address in my notebook.

IV. Health.

I wasn't getting any younger and I wasn't exactly in the best physical shape.

When I came inside with the grilled burgers Minttu was chopping the cucumber so quickly that I stopped in surprise.

'Be careful!' I called. 'Don't cut a finger!'

'I do this every day,' she said, rolling her eyes at me.

Oh. She must help to prepare meals. I went up to tell Elias we had some food if he was hungry, but he was so engrossed with his game that he only mumbled acknowledgement and never came down.

When I returned to the kitchen Minttu showed me the bowl of salad with an expectant look on her face. I gave her a casual thumbs-up and she dropped her gaze to look blankly at the salad.

'Thank you!' I said hurriedly. 'That looks fantastic; much better than I could do. Good job!'

Now the smile was back on her face.

Praise is important to her, I thought. Remember that.

After dinner Minttu and I resumed playing Minecraft. We finished our big treehouse and built a spiral staircase running up inside the massive trunk. She assumed the role of teacher and helper, explaining how this world worked and taking care of me. When I did something stupid, like falling out of the treehouse, both of us laughed.

Okay, I thought. Kids aren't so bad. This is kind of cool.

5

I woke up thirsty around midnight. In the twilight of the Nordic summer night I stumbled downstairs, yawning, clad only in my underwear. Half way down the stairs I stopped in surprise. I had expected the kids to be asleep in their upstairs bedrooms, but Minttu was sitting on the couch wrapped in a bathrobe playing on a tablet computer. She looked up at me in shock, pulled her robe tighter and slowly curled up into a ball.

We stared at each other and the look on her face shook me. She was terrified. She thought I was sneaking down in the middle of the night to molest her or something. Here she was, almost alone with a near-naked foreign man she barely knew. I expected her to scream for Elias, but she seemed frozen in terror. Not knowing what else to do, I yawned and smiled in what I hoped was a disarming manner and mumbled something about being thirsty. I tried to saunter into the kitchen like walking around in my underwear was completely normal.

Finns are cool about nudity, right? I frantically tried to reassure myself as I gulped down a glass of water. Europeans think nudity is no big deal, unlike uptight Americans. Holy shit, if I had walked in front of a young girl in my underwear in America I would have been arrested for corrupting a minor or exposing myself or something.

I stared at my empty glass and realised I had another problem. Now I had to walk through the living room again. I listened, but it didn't sound like Minttu had run up the stairs where she could lock herself in her room or go to her cousin for protection. She must still be sitting there, praying that the almost-nude foreign guy in her kitchen wasn't going to hurt her. I put the glass down and took a deep breath.

As nonchalantly as I could I strolled through the living room to the stairs. Out of the corner of my eye I saw Minttu watching me out of the corner of her eye.

6

The next morning I found the little girl asleep on the couch under a pile of puppies. I wondered if she had been afraid to come upstairs to her bedroom next to where I was sleeping and had needed comfort and reassurance from the dogs. Perhaps, but when she woke there didn't seem to be a hint of that night-time terror of me.

'Are you taking Santeri and Freyja out?' Minttu asked cheerfully, wiping the sleep from her eyes. 'Let me get dressed so I can come!'

Okay, I thought, I passed the test. The episode last night had scared her, but something good had come out of it. Now she trusts me. She knows I won't hurt her.

'Yeah, let's go!' I said. 'It's a beautiful day!'

During the day and a half Elias and Minttu were there Elias stayed upstairs in his room, door closed, playing his online games. He didn't come out to eat or go to the bathroom or anything, as far as I could tell. Minttu, on the other hand, never left my side. We did everything together, from walking the puppies to cooking to playing video games. We went to the store to buy ice creams and eat them on the walk back. After an hour we decided to go back to the store and do it again. We laughed and joked and helped each other with our native languages. I knew next to nothing about the Finnish education system and Minttu patiently explained how her school worked and what she was studying. Elias walked to their grandparents' as soon as he awoke, but Minttu waited until late afternoon, the last possible moment before she left.

'Do you want me to walk you to your grandparents?'

'I ride my bike.'

'I can still walk next to you if you want.'

'You don't need to. Bye!'

Helmet on her head, she waved and closed the door behind her. I didn't like her riding down the streets to her grandparents alone. Finland is a safe place and we were in a safe neighbourhood. It was in the middle of the afternoon with dozens of people around, and she was only going a few blocks to her grandparents, a route she probably took all the time. But still I didn't like it.

I paced the floor, imagining her peddling her way so I could guess when she arrived. But then my imagination took a dark turn. I saw a man jumping out of bushes, clamping a hand over her mouth and dragging her away. He didn't have a face. The abandoned bicycle lay on its side, the back wheel still futilely turning. The vision was so real I was certain it was actually happening. I opened the front door, started to sprint after her route and hopped to a painful halt. I had forgotten my fucking knee. Minttu was being carried off as I limped around like a crippled old man. I was useless, hopeless, worthless.

But wait: there might be a faster way. Standing on one leg, I pulled the phone from my pocket and frantically opened the contacts app. During my marriage I had been responsible for keeping the contact information for everyone in the family. Yet now I couldn't remember the name of Mari's dad. I glanced around at my surroundings, hoping something would trigger my memory. Trees, bushes, sidewalk, the bike stand with an empty slot for Minttu's missing bike, nothing. In desperation I typed 'Mari's dad' in the app and was flabbergasted when it popped up. That was exactly how I had saved his number. A deep, cheerful, older man's voice answered.

'Is Minttu okay?' I practically yelled at him.

'Mitä?'

'Is Minttu there?'

Pause. 'Minttu?'

Yes, that's his voice, but I had forgotten he didn't speak a word of English. I took a few deep breaths to calm down and think. I had to remember the words. If someone was dragging her away right now as I was fumbling with this stupid language…

'Minä olen David. Onko…Minttu…sinun…koti?'

'Oi, hei David! Joo, joo, Elias ja Minttu ovat täällä…' he said, followed by a long string of words I couldn't understand. In the background I heard people calling to each other and bumping around as they packed the car to go to the summer cabin. There was a little girl's laugh.

My diaphragm relaxed and I exhaled deeply into the phone and his ear.

'Okay. Thanks! Kiitos!' I said, and hung up.

I fulfilled my responsibility to watch my friend's kid, I thought. But that wasn't how I felt. It wasn't the satisfaction of completing a task; it was relief that she was safe.

Now I wandered the empty house, suddenly detesting that silence which I had so craved. I looked at the PlayStation controllers we had left on the couch. They seemed abandoned, lost. Like me. I'm lonely, I realised. This is what I've felt ever since I moved into my new flat, but I didn't recognise it until now. Maybe I don't need to keep wondering how to live again, I thought. Maybe what I had just experienced was living. With nothing else to do, I played Minecraft alone and thought.

7

The happiness and optimism from my brief time with Minttu stayed with me even after Kaarle and Mari came home from their holiday and I returned to my lonely bachelor flat. For the first time in months, maybe years, I felt hope for my future. I had a plan.

Money is the foundation of modern life, so the first thing I needed was to stabilise my financial situation. What kind of relationships did homeless people have? How many books have they written?

I opened up every one of those letters on my keyboard

drawer. There were more than fifty of them, and the floor next to my chair was covered in ragged envelopes. In a notebook I meticulously listed all my creditors and how much I owed them. I tapped away on my antique Hewlett Packard 10B Business calculator and stared at the final result.

Holy shit, I thought. If someone handed me ten thousand euros it would not make the slightest difference.

Briefly my mind daydreamed of a quick fix. Winning the lottery. Discovering a briefcase filled with 500-euro bills abandoned in the bushes by a spooked drug dealer. Being named the heir of a rich relative, both newly discovered and newly deceased.

Angrily I pushed those thoughts away. They were less than helpful; they were dangerous. Not addressing my problems by fleeing reality was how I got to this point. I had written books one word at a time; I would fix this one euro at a time. That was priority number one, so selling myself as a writer was where I put all my focus and energies. I carefully made lists of goals—not of results, but of things I could actually control. I would work a minimum of twelve hours a day, every day. There were no such things as weekends or coffee breaks. Time not working, like eating lunch or running errands, would not count.

By the third day I realised traditional journalism was dead. People wanted their news for free and haemorrhaging newspapers could not buy work from freelancers. Websites graciously offered to let me write articles for 'exposure' instead of pay. I didn't bother to ask my landlords if they would let me pay my rent in 'exposure' because I knew their answer.

Instead I turned to companies and organisations. They needed press releases, articles for their internal newsletters, stories for their web pages. Now that the Finnish economy was finally improving after years of malaise companies had money to spend and ministries had stable budgets. Because the domestic markets in the Nordic area are so small, companies look abroad for growth.

The international language of business is English, so companies needed me or someone like me.

I wrote a simple introductory email, detailing what I could do and why they should choose me. I kept it so short that the reader would not have to scroll to read it all. I was fanatical. After I ran out of Finnish companies I moved to Swedish companies. When I ran out of them I went through Estonian and Norwegian businesses. When Norway began to dry up I returned to Finnish corporations and started all over again.

In Finland the only thing that matters is how you fit into society. This is true everywhere, but Finland is so small and homogenous that the line between in and out is clear and inviolate, not easily passed even by the most dedicated foreigner. To be accepted as a potential writer I had to prove that I was accepted as a writer by Finnish society, and for this nothing was better than citing my Nokia book.

Now every recipient of my email could visualise where I fit in. Oh, this is the guy who wrote that book about Nokia, they thought. He must be able to write. He must have lots of contacts in the technology sector and probably lots of businesspeople trust him. Now we know how he fits into Finnish society. Now we know who he is, and if we need something written we'll call him.

And they did.

I began contacting people as soon as they returned from their summer holidays. By the time the birch leaves started to change colour to their sickly yellow I was writing half of the time and marketing myself the other half. When the leaves covered the ground I barely had any time for marketing. I had strict goals for the number of cold calls and cold emails to make, so I had to eat in front of my computer in order to hit my targets. I eventually topped out at 4,904 companies when I had to stop contacting them. I had so much work to do I couldn't handle any more clients.

Throughout the autumn orders poured in from communication agencies, government ministries, NGOs and corporations. My name began to be passed around, and I was contacted by people and companies I had never heard of. I doubled my writing and editing rates, but the demand did not slow.

I took my phone off silent mode and answered every call from bill collectors. I told them frankly how much money was currently in my account and how much money I would be receiving and when. How much would they like today, and when would they like the remainder? They seemed amused that I took control of the conversation and even used their favourite tactic: detailing the situation and asking: 'What are we going to do about this?'

By the end of two months I was completely caught up on my bills. Not a single cent had been written off as uncollectable. My plan had worked so well I made more challenging goals for myself. By the end of the year that once insurmountable pile of debt had been cut by a third. I began to tentatively buy things I needed, like socks, and I even splurged on new vacuum cleaner bags. I put a new bag in my elderly vacuum and gave an experimental pass or two on my tattered throw rug. The vacuum worked better and even sounded better. I turned it off and looked at my feet in their new socks on the freshly cleaned rug.

Why did I waste that money? I wondered. The old bag still worked. I could have just emptied it again.

8

My phone beeped. It was Kaarle.

'What are you doing for Christmas?'

'No plans,' I typed back. 'Probably editing an article.'

'Would you like to have Christmas with us?'

I had avoided thinking about Christmas. Christmas was a time for family and I had no family in Finland. Now suddenly that closed door was open and I delightedly burst through it.

'Yes, I would like to spend Christmas with you. I'll make my famous Joululimppu.'

A few days afterwards I received a call from Robert, asking if

I wanted to spend Christmas with him and his family. I told him that I had already accepted another invitation, but thanked him for the invite. This was entirely unexpected. Two people had invited me to Christmas. Some people not only knew about my outsider existence, but had taken the effort of reaching out to me. There was an opportunity there, if I only knew how to grasp it.

In the grey afternoon of Christmas Eve Kaarle was outside Mari's parents' flat waiting for me. I had remembered where they lived because Minttu had pointed it out back in July. Inside was his wife Mari's family, people I had met before at irregular events. As the host, Mari's father said hello and shook my sweaty hand. Cousins and siblings and kids moved about the room, doing what people do at Christmas, trying not to stare.

It was clear that I had been discussed. You remember David, right? He is that abandoned foreigner with no family. We should invite him to Christmas. It would be nice for him not to be alone during the holidays, and it would be a good example for the kids to think about the unfortunate.

It was a gracious gesture, something they didn't have to do, and I suddenly wanted no part of it. I laid my coat reluctantly on the floor right next to the door where I could get to it easily and handed over my homemade Finnish Christmas bread for it to disappear into the kitchen.

The adults were gathered in a few small groups, speaking incomprehensible Finnish. The kids were in a larger amorphous mass, constantly breaking apart and reforming as they played, yelling sounds which had no meaning to me. I looked from one mystery conversation to the next. Occasionally the speaker would make eye contact with me and quickly looked away. I shrank against the wall and Kaarle looked at me unhappily. He wanted to make me feel at ease but didn't know what to do. I didn't either.

Why had Kaarle invited me here? Didn't he know how out of place I would be? I don't belong here. They drop a foreigner who can't speak a word of the language into a tight-knit family. It's like he wanted to make me uncomfortable, the fucker. But I couldn't have refused, because that would have been rude. He put me in an impossible position, and he should have known better. I wondered how I could tell him this tactfully, but my angry musings were interrupted.

'David, come here!'

The high-pitched, heavily-accented English of a little girl cut through the Finno-Ugric confusion like a horn at a hockey game. Minttu waved at me to come sit next to her on the couch. She wanted to show me a compilation of funny animal videos on her phone. She had it queued up as if she had been waiting for me to arrive. We sat on the couch and she kept looking at my face for my reaction, so I fake laughed at the appropriate parts and tried to think of some way to leave without hurting everyone's feelings. They were doing something nice, inviting this lonely outsider into their homes and giving him a Christmas. I decided when Minttu's video was over I would claim a sudden headache and go home. Everyone would be relieved.

But before the videos were over Kaarle waved me into the kitchen. They had already eaten, but there was still plenty of food available. I used to love the Finnish Christmas dinner and looked over the ransacked kitchen. Cold ham (although I still preferred American-style ham, steaming hot out of the oven); smoked and salted salmon; potatoes; faux caviar; hard-boiled eggs; swede, carrot and liver casseroles; pickled herring; rossoli; my lonely loaf of bread; and for dessert Christmas star pastries and home cheese.

For the first time Christmas dinner didn't appeal to me. I was late and would eat awkwardly alone. I unenthusiastically followed my tradition and gathered a little bit of everything and placed my plate on the table. I glanced up at the cabinets and noticed Minttu was peeking into the kitchen.

'Here are glasses,' she said, coming in and opening a cabinet.

'Thanks; kiitos,' I said, smiling at her.

Minttu got a Christmas star and sat down next to me. She

slowly nibbled it, timing it so that she finished her pastry when I finished my plate.

'I like Christmas stars,' I told her.

'I like them too. I baked some at home. It was fun.'

'You'll have to show me how to make them someday. I like to bake too.'

I started to relax. I wasn't eating alone. If an adult had sat down to keep me company it would have been forced and awkward, but kids are so genuine. She was there because she wanted to be there, not because it was a social obligation or she felt like she should do a good deed during the holidays.

Minttu had decided to become my hostess and make me feel at home, and she was good at it. She seemed to immediately know whatever I might need. If I glanced questioningly down a hallway she guessed I was looking for the bathroom and showed me where it was. If I poured a cup of coffee and went to the refrigerator she appeared at my elbow to explain someone had left the milk behind me on the counter. When I sat alone she immediately sat next to me. The only time she left my side to be with the other kids was when Santa Claus made his appearance. While Santa was handing out gifts I watched from my lonely place on the stairs and missed her keenly.

I had been in Finland for ten years but this was the first time I had seen a Joulupukki handing out gifts. The American Santa is an idealistic figure. He has a blindingly white beard, is luxuriously fat, and looks as perfect as a meticulously drawn cartoon. The Finnish Santa is more earthy. He is half-starved, has a grey beard, and his clothes seem as if he has been sleeping under a pine tree on a bed of moss. The American Santa appears in the middle of the night like a dream, but the Finnish Santa strolls into your house in front of everyone in the grey winter daylight. It was apt how the two cultures view the world. Americans are idealistic and irrationally cheery, while Finns are pragmatic.

Joulupukki posed for pictures with the children, with the

youngest cousin playing his traditional role and flipping out in terror. Santa was calm and handled the twisting and screaming toddler professionally. He handed out gifts from an old bag and bantered with the kids. I had no idea what he was saying, but it looked like he knew what he was doing.

As I watched from my solitary perch on the stairs Kaarle sauntered over. He had kept an eye on Minttu and me the entire day but had mostly left us alone. I had now relaxed enough to be able to chat with him semi-normally—when are you going back to work? I hear we might have snow next week—but without Minttu I could feel the loneliness and anxiety beginning to creep back. When Santa left and she returned to show me her haul Kaarle quietly melted away, leaving us to try out the toys Santa had brought her.

9

'Would you like a ride home?'

Kaarle's voice cut through our game, and I looked up in surprise from where I was sitting on the floor with Minttu. Through the windows I could see burning streetlights and a black sky.

'I didn't realise it was so late,' I told him. 'Sure, I'd love a ride home if it is not a problem.'

All six of us piled into Kaarle and Mari's van. Nea and Niilo had ignored me for their more interesting cousins, but now that the cousins were no longer around I became an object of curiosity. Minttu shooed them away. She demanded that I sit next to her and was ready to trounce her little brother and sister if they thought otherwise. As we drove down the black, shiny wet roads Minttu showed me funny pictures on her Instagram feed. I had only used the service to follow a few friends and Formula One stars, but she had found all kinds of interesting accounts which I hadn't known had existed.

'I like these cooking and animal accounts,' I said. 'I'm on

Instagram too, but you seem to know more about it than I do.'

'Give me your phone,' she said. 'We can send messages to each other.'

She took my phone and I watched as she made my account follow hers.

I had had a lot of fun with Minttu back during the summer when we spent a day together. She had really saved Christmas for me, too. I had been so lonely and awkward and she simply barged in and took over. She had made me laugh, feel at home and feel welcomed, something none of the adults could do, even though they had tried. They knew how much of an outsider I was but were powerless to do anything about it. Minttu, with her sweet innocence and genuine affection, had strolled through my wall of self-imposed isolation like it didn't exist. I had thought these episodes with Minttu were one-offs, events which were now over, but she was under the impression that we were beginning a friendship.

Okay, I thought, I'm willing.

'May I be friends with Minttu on Instagram?' I called up to Kaarle, who was driving the van.

He looked at me in the rear-view mirror. 'I didn't even know she had an account,' he said. I couldn't see his mouth, but his eyes were not smiling.

10

I was on Tinder for about two minutes when the thought of Heljä crashed into my head like a rogue wave. She had used hook up apps to cheat on me, and the thought of stumbling across her picture was too much.

Don't be stupid, a part of me said. Why would she be on Tinder if she has a boyfriend?

Why was she on Tinder if she had a husband? another part of me asked.

This was a question I didn't want to explore. I deleted my

profile and deleted the app.

Instead I contacted a young woman I knew, a former friend of Heljä's and a free spirit whom I had always liked. I hadn't seen her since the wedding, although I had been in contact with her irregularly over the years. She had a young girl now but after chatting with her on messaging apps I was happy to see that she hadn't changed. Yet she was about a four-hour train ride away. She was willing to get together, but also brought up the distance between us. She only came to Helsinki about once a year. Would I have to take a whole day off work every time I wanted to get laid? The simple logistics were not very suitable for either of us, so we mutually dropped the idea.

My other options were bars, clubs and acquaintances. I felt tired just thinking about all the effort that would entail. But there was a simpler alternative to get what I wanted. An internet search led me to a thriving Helsinki marketplace for sex workers.

Some of the women were faceless. A few had photos of them cut off at the neck, while other more enterprising ones covered their faces with black holes of nothingness or cutesy emojis. A number of photos appeared to be heavily manipulated to cut out double chins, make boobs a bit bigger or waists a bit narrower. Many of their posts were in English: a high percentage of Finland's sex workers are foreigners.

I glanced through the girls, occasionally opening up a profile to study one more closely. Gradually I realised I was looking for a skinny Finn. I didn't want a Ukrainian or Estonian.

The one I picked had dyed blond hair, brown eyes and cultivated a sexy and fun demeanour. She was expensive and busy. Two hundred and fifty euros for an hour, and it took a few attempts to find a mutually convenient time. Sofie was the name she used. I didn't know how this was supposed to work, so she told me to meet her at a club downtown.

I arrived early, like I do with all my appointments, so bought a beer and kept an eye on the door. The beer had no effect because

I was so nervous. Sofie arrived a few minutes late and I recognised her immediately. She was twenty-four, according to her bio, but I suspected she might be a few years older. She was tiny, dressed like a young woman on a night out instead of a stereotypical hooker. She caught me studying her and smiled as I approached.

'Hi, I'm David,' I said stupidly. I guess Johns are supposed to use fake names, like John. What did they use in Finland? Jussi? Johan?

'Hi, I'm Sofie,' said Sofie. 'Do you want to get a drink?'

I glanced at the crowded, dark, noisy bar. I'm too old for this.

'Or we could go straight to my place. It's an Airbnb,' she explained. 'A lot of the girls use them.'

I nodded, relieved. I hadn't wanted to get a hotel room or bring her back to my flat. Apparently somewhere to fuck is included in the price.

'First things first,' she said, and I blinked at her before I understood she was talking about her money.

'Right here? Now?'

'Of course. It's legal, you know, as long as there are no third parties involved.'

Hoping that an online forum didn't constitute a third party, I dug the bills out of my wallet and handed them to her. They disappeared instantly. I didn't think she put them in her small bag, but I struggled to figure out where else she would have stuffed them.

'Ready?' Sofie asked, and we started walking down the sidewalk.

She bumped against my left arm as we walked and I realised that she was offering her arm if I wanted to take it. I was like a sixteen-year-old on his first date and frozen with fear, so after a couple of bumps she settled into a companionly walk by my side, her heels clicking on the sidewalk.

Sofie checked me out as we walked, talking and studying and judging me, making sure I was a safe trick. I was nervous and clueless and hoped she didn't interpret this as a plotting serial killer. We walked a number of blocks and went into a rather nice, old building with high ceilings and gleaming stone floors and chipped marble steps. It even had one of those tiny old elevators with protruding, worn buttons and accordion-style finger-smasher iron doors. Her flat was on the third floor.

'Do you like what you do?' I asked.

'Hell yes,' she said. 'I like to fuck, I'm my own boss and make good money.'

I was disappointed. This was the stock answer, but what did I expect? This was a business transaction and she was a professional. She answered like she was supposed to answer, just like all those hundreds of corporate interviews I had done. I knew exactly what a CEO would say before he opened his mouth, just like I knew what she would say. But I was dissatisfied and decided to push.

'Really?' I asked. 'There isn't anything else you would rather be doing?'

'I'm building a mobile payment app,' Sofie said. 'Think of an orgy between Paypal, Mobile Pay and Bitcoin.'

'That's cool. Maybe I'll see you pitching at Slush.'

Underneath the smiling theatre mask of her face she was careful, evaluating me.

'I'm just curious,' I said. 'I used to chat with the girls at stripclubs like this too. I know you have a story, but I'm not trying to save you. I'm not even trying to save myself.'

'I don't need saved.'

I shrugged. 'Do people ever hire you just for companionship?'

'All the time. A few of my regulars do that, and we rarely have sex.'

'Well, you're nice to be with, but I want to have sex.'

She laughed. 'What's your kink? What do you like?'

'Speak Finnish.'

'Suomi ei ole seksikäs kieli!'

No, it wasn't. Finnish is the least sexy language on the planet.

Its sexiness, or lack thereof, was not why I wanted her to speak it.

Sofie sat me down on the edge of the bed, turned on some music, and came to me with a crooked grin on her face. She moved slowly, but rhythmically, peeling off one item of clothing after another. It was sweet just to be inside a woman again, but as it went on I got rougher, more needy, more desperate, as she faux panted Jumala, Jumala. I pinned her arms above her head when I came.

Well, that was paying for sex. It was exciting, in a way. It was also more than a little sad. I had to pay for it because I couldn't handle developing a normal relationship with a woman. I climbed off her and walked into the bathroom.

'Don't flush your condom! It's bad for the environment!' Sofie called. 'Throw it in the trash.'

Everything was hyper clear to my senses. I pulled off the condom and stepped on the lever for the little metal trash can. Its lid smacked against the bathroom wall and the sound of the echo merged with the initial reverberating bang. There was a new bag in the trash can. With no garbage to hold it down the bag was almost level with the top of the container. I pushed it down, the bag crackling, and dropped in the condom. It hit the bag with a miniscule sound like a soft exhalation. I tried and failed to take my foot off the lever gently, causing a muffled bang of two cheap pieces of metal hitting each other with plastic in between.

'You were good,' I told Sofie, walking back into the bedroom. 'I'm happy.'

'Good,' she said lightly, but she continued to carefully study me. The real danger for a prostitute was after sex.

'I'd like to see you again if you're willing,' I said, putting on my clothes.

'Of course! You have my number.'

What was I supposed to do now? A hug and a kiss were out of the question, but it was impossible for me to leave without some sort of ritual closure. Not being able to think of anything else I stuck out my hand like we had just concluded a business deal, which I guess we had.

'Thanks again,' I told her. 'I appreciate it.'

'Kiitos!' she said, and hurried me out the front door.

The deadlock clicked a shattered second after she closed the door. Instead of taking the elevator I walked down the worn, graceful marble stairs in their half circles. The old, heavy wooden door had been modified with a buzzer and it took me a few seconds to find the green button in the darkness. Auki, I thought, open, and walked out into the cold, moist, melancholic Helsinki air.

I walked all the way to Rautatientori and the bus stop next to the big yellow central post office building. I had to wait a long time for the bus. Down the shiny wet street were the cabs in their coiled row, picking up a steady stream of rowdy pre-New Year partiers. Their faint yells and laughter floated up the street to me. I might have taken a taxi, but couldn't stand the thought of talking to the driver and telling him where I wanted to go. I'd rather just wait in the cold for the impersonal and voiceless interaction with the bus driver.

The bus finally arrived and I sat in my regular place, in the back on the right where I could look out the window. As we were crossing the old draw-bridge to Lauttasaari I hit the red button and got off on the first stop on the island. It was a long way from my flat but I wanted to walk.

I followed the winding paths and sidewalks running along the southeast coast of Lauttasaari. As I walked past the harbours I heard creaks in the darkness. It was almost January and all of the boats had been taken out of the water for the freeze, but still I heard ropes gently creaking on wood. Ghost ships. The bright lights of Ruoholahti and Jätkäsaari shined across the bay, seemingly brighter than the lonely street lights under which I walked.

There were thousands of people over there in the heart of the city. What was Sofie doing now? Checking her phone for her next appointment, sobbing in a corner, laughing at me, contentedly playing some mobile game? How did she feel? There were others, too, behind those bright lights. People I had met, or worked with, or had interacted with in some fashion. Dozens of people. Maybe hundreds. All fading away, decomposing with time, their remembered faces and voices getting fainter and fainter. Maybe Heljä was over there. What was she doing now? Did she ever think about me?

It didn't matter. Nothing mattered. What did the poet say? Borrowed time and borrowed world and borrowed eyes with which to sorrow it.

The black sea heaved softly, like a living thing contemplating its own reality and ignoring the world of men. It was so inviting. The sea rejected no one and no thing. It would accept you and enfold you into itself without the slightest hesitation. Step in and immerse yourself into the world's amniotic fluid as it was in the beginning, is now and ever shall be, world without end.

I stopped walking and shook my leg a few times. That didn't help, so I reached into my pockets and tried to rearrange myself. Her vaginal fluids were drying in my pubic hair. It was uncomfortable, but there was nothing to do about it here. I needed to get into the water.

I needed to get into the water.

11

The new year finally brought a little snow to drab and desolate Helsinki. The white on the ground did wonders, reflecting back the miniscule sunlight which could work its way through the clouds. The bare trees and rocks of the shoreline of Lauttasaari suddenly looked inviting with a blanket of snow. Within a few weeks, I knew from experience, the gargantuan blanket of clouds would dissipate and we would experience the blue sky and bright sun again.

My drinking fluctuated. I might go two or three weeks

without touching a drop, and then the urge would hit so strong I broke and bought a bottle of whisky. My first shot was after my morning shower and coffee. I knew it wasn't healthy to be buzzed by eight in the morning. I berated myself, but couldn't stop while there was still whisky in my apartment. I finished off a bottle and would be dry for the next couple of weeks.

Every day I found time to walk. Sometimes I wandered north along the shore, where I looked longingly at the sauna association building among the trees or circled hurriedly around the police summer cabin. That inbred American distrust of the police was still there, and I didn't want any cops to take notice of me.

At other times I went south through the little park and one day the sea was so low that a narrow spit of sand connected the main island to its little brother, the islet of Sisä-Hattu. The islet was mostly rock, with a few stunted trees and blueberry bushes in the centre. The wind off the sea had blown the snow off bare stone, revealing names and figures carved by people a hundred years ago as they waited for ships to arrive. I looked at initials in hearts and wondered how those loves had turned out. I tried to decipher the strange, delicate words in poems and imaged someone tapping away with hammer and chisel, occasionally looking to the horizon for the appearance of tiny white sails.

Once I discovered a makeshift shrine on the shore, composed of a few burned out grave candles and withered flowers. I stopped and considered the memorial and turned to look out to sea. I knew why it was here, because it was at the same remote place I had myself chosen. A body sinking through the cold water to softly hit the bottom in a cloud of sediment. Dirt between my teeth. Would anyone light candles for me? Don't be stupid, I thought. Who would do so? For what purpose?

In time I came to recognise people. Joggers and dog-walkers and bored perambulators there were in plenty, but there were also different people. Lone men and women, ranging in ages from teenager to geriatric, wandering the streets and paths of

Lauttasaari. There was the Hippy, an immaculate older lady in expensive clothes on an expensive bike who did yoga and caressed trees on the shoreline. The Searcher was a young overweight man who always appeared to be looking for something lost as he walked, his eyes scanning the ground left and right. Widow's Peak never wore a hat, no matter what the weather, and even in the bitterest cold contented himself with a light jacket. Blondie had a rhythmic, bouncy walk which made me think she had danced once upon a time. There is nothing in the world sadder than a former dancer.

We never spoke, but as the months passed they came to recognise me, too. I called our mode of recognition the Nod. It was brief eye contact and a simple nod of the head, made to each other as we passed, yet it encompassed a depth of communication and understanding. I see you, it said. I know you and why you are out here, walking alone in the rain and flurries and mud. I am just like you. I had no idea there were so many of us. We were everywhere.

12

My plan to have concrete goals had worked so well that I decided to expand it. I maintained my frenetic freelance writing schedule but added tasks for mental and physical health. I started meditating again after a decade of inactivity. My left knee had been sore and weak for months after that little stumble with the dogs at Kaarle's, so I included tasks to get back in shape. I put strict limits on the nicotine, ate three pieces of fresh fruit a day and started exercising.

The first day I could only do three push-ups without a rest, but I persevered and put in a mini regime of push-ups, sit-ups and squats. The next morning I was so sore that I couldn't sit up but had to roll out of bed. My left knee protested against the squats, quivering and threatening to collapse, so I bought a knee brace. I kept it up, despite the initial awkwardness and pain, and exercised every weekday besides rare occasions where my schedule wouldn't allow it.

My finances had improved so much that I let my housing benefit expire. I understood that I had enjoyed the benefits of Finnish society through things like the public transportation network and health care, but this monthly deposit into my bank account had been concrete and for my benefit alone. I had looked at the transactions in my account and imagined a person or a company paying that in taxes, which now had come to me. Finland had invested in me, and now I could return the favour. I was making enough money that a significant portion of my income was going to taxes. I kept a pro rata estimate of my income taxes, and as my earnings increased I jumped enough tax brackets to feel justified in complaining about my tax burden.

As my birthday approached I became apprehensive. I had no one to celebrate it with. No one would throw a party for me or invite me out for drinks or stop by with a gift or even give me a call. I didn't want to sit by myself in my tiny apartment and think about how no one cared, so I developed a clever idea. I would travel to Sicily for my birthday and then could tell myself that the reason no one came to visit me was because I wasn't available. On the morning of 25 March I sat alone on the stone bleachers of the ancient Greek theatre at Taormina and stared at smoking Mount Etna in the distance. I had no one to share the beautiful sight with, but at least I wasn't in damp, dreary Helsinki waiting for the knock on the door which would never come. You didn't reject me, I told the crowd of acquaintances in my mind, I rejected you.

A reminder of the good old days came when Chris, my best friend from America, finally joined Facebook. He had been a neighbour growing up and we had been friends since about the age of ten. I had been the best man at his wedding, and he had been the best man at mine. Everyday we sent private messages to each other, talking about books, dreaming up flamboyant insults or playing our favourite game of 'how much?':

'You're in a phone booth with a very unamused tom cat,' Chris wrote. 'You got an industrial rubber glove on ur left hand

and needle nose pliers in ur right. You gotta pull 2 of the cats fangs out. How much?’

’You’re going to look like an anatomical drawing in a biology textbook with all your muscles and organs exposed when that tom cat is done with you,’ I replied. ’30 million.’

Yet being in contact with Chris also reminded me how much had changed. Deep in the American presidential campaign I posted on Facebook that Donald Trump was the worst qualified candidate in living memory. This infuriated Chris, and he punished me with a flurry of virulent alt-right memes. I remained silent, Chris calmed down, and we returned to friendly insults and jokes.

I heard more from Robert as well. That cry for help when I asked to go ice fishing continued to be answered as time passed. Robert’s activities followed the Finnish seasons and he invited me to participate with him. When it was time to plant his garden he asked me to come out to his house to the west of Helsinki and get my hands dirty. When the perch began to migrate, or the first mushroom appeared, or moose hunting season opened, I would get a call from him. I was often busy and tried to schedule more convenient times, but Robert firmly rebuked me.

‘That isn’t how it works,’ he told me. ‘The Finnish lakes, forests and seas decide when we go, not you. We take what they offer when they offer it.’

When the spring herring season opened I rode a bus to the train station to go meet him. As I crossed Lauttasaari bridge I saw about thirty herring fishers lining the side. If I had only wanted herring I could have fished right here, I thought, but it isn’t herring that I’m looking for. I needed to be out in Finnish nature with a friend. The herring were secondary.

When the urge struck me I contacted Sofie. I preferred off-peak times, like Thursday evenings. I scheduled myself so strictly that I only allowed a half hour to travel, an hour with Sofie, and a half hour to travel back, and I would have to make up my time getting laid by working into the night.

She relaxed a bit with me as I became a regular customer, and we always chatted before or after sex. We talked about food, or music, or the economy. I told her things I had learned through my articles which I thought she would be interested in, such as new mobile payment technology. Sofie smiled at me wistfully and I realised she wasn't working on her payment app anymore, or perhaps she had never worked on it. This made me sad for some reason I couldn't pin down.

'Who do you vote for?' I asked her once.

'The Greens, and sometimes Vasemmisto.'

'I like Li Andersson.'

Sofie looked at me in surprise. 'You don't seem the leftist type,' she said.

'I'm not, but I like her. She stands by her convictions but is also realistic. So many of the fringe parties fail because they are inflexible about their ideologies.'

'Foreigners never support the parties in their best interests. They vote for parties which hate foreigners, just to try and show they belong.'

'Or they don't vote at all because they feel they don't belong,' I said.

'Those are only the weak ones, but they are a majority,' she said.

Sofie's keen insight both disturbed and angered me. I told her to speak Finnish again as I fucked her, and she did so, but more mocking and challenging than normal. I couldn't understand all she was saying, and I suspect it was cruel, but I didn't care. Our professional relationship had advanced to the point where we could safely despise each other. I used her and she used me and we were both fine with it. What else are relationships for than to use each other and discard them when they were no longer profitable? It was one of the best orgasms I had had in years.

Through it all the craving for alcohol remained. Sometimes it was dormant for weeks, but it never disappeared. I would break on occasion and go to Alko to buy a bottle of whisky. I forced myself to wait until I was home to start drinking, although I desperately wanted to take my first gulp right there at the register. I needed to hide it. I was ashamed and didn't want people to know.

Only once did I open up about my alcohol problem. I was at a meeting of an English-speaking association, and we always closed with a formal round of toasts. When Jaakko came to offer me a glass of wine, I stared at it and shook my head.

'I can't,' I said. 'After the divorce I needed three or four shots every morning just to function. I can't touch it.'

Jaakko put a compassionate hand on my shoulder and five or six other members stared at me in silent horror. I did our toasts with a glass of water. On the bus ride home I got off one stop early to go to Alko.

13

'Beep!'

Every morning when I turned on my phone I was greeted by a cheerful notification sound.

'Good morning, David!' I read.

'Good morning, Minttu!' I replied. 'What are you doing today?'

Minttu and I stayed in close contact via messaging apps. I discovered her likes and dislikes and she learned mine. I helped her with English and she helped me with Finland. She explained different aspects of Finnish culture and society which I had never understood, even though I had been married to a Finn for almost a decade. I also re-learned things from her. I re-learned the naïve optimism of youth and the strange idea that perhaps someone actually liked me. I tried to insulate myself from this idea, and pretend it wasn't true, so as to avoid the inevitable pain when it ended. I knew it would end, as all things do.

Minttu told me what she was doing in school, complained about how Nea and Niilo were annoying, and forwarded funny videos. I enjoyed that she shared her everyday life with me, from photos of the dogs to recipes of things she liked to cook. Once she sent me a screenshot of two large flowers she built in Minecraft. One was red and one was pink. Red was my favourite colour and pink was hers.

She created a private group in Instagram which consisted of her four closest friends from school and me. I'm sure that being a 40-something man in a private online group with 12-year-old girls put me on all sorts of government watch lists, but I didn't mind. I was deeply touched and honoured that Minttu put me in the same category as her best friends.

Kaarle and Mari had three kids in their family but still lived in a modest flat in Vantaa. Like a growing hermit crab the family was ready for a new shell. They found a 1970s ranch-style house out in the country on the east side of Helsinki. They would have much more space in the house, a huge fenced-in yard and forest for the dogs, a garage and storage shed and even a wood-burning sauna, but perhaps the main reason they chose it was because it was only fifteen minutes from the harbour where they kept their boat.

Kaarle summoned a throng of his friends and family to help them move, including me. As always in these gatherings I kept my mouth shut and my head down. Everyone spoke Finnish and ignored me, only talking to me in English if I showed my ignorance, like taking boxes to the wrong room. About half-way through we stopped to eat lunch. Everyone was babbling in Finnish and I sat silently listening, but suddenly something caught my attention.

'Ajetaan David kotiin Fucker kanssa,' Kaarle said to Mari.

Mari started to reply but I loudly interrupted.

'You know, it's funny when you can't understand what people are saying but you hear your name and "fucker" in the same sentence,' I said.

Most of them roared with laughter. Elias choked on his pizza and was on the verge of spitting it out on his plate before he managed to swallow it.

'I'm really sorry,' Kaarle said, who hadn't laughed. 'I was saying that I could take you home with our old car. We named it Fucker because it gives us a lot of problems.'

I waved it off, finished my pizza and got back to carrying boxes while the others were still talking and eating. A few hours later it was over. The supposedly big strong men were lying around in states of utter exhaustion while indefatigable Mari was still putting beds and tables back together and organising things. Kaarle's mother Kirsti arrived with the three kids. She had been keeping them out of the way at her place during the move.

Nea walked in the door and stopped when she saw me sitting alone in a corner. The look of surprise on her face changed to utter delight and she ran shrieking to me with outstretched arms, not even bothering to follow the cardinal commandment of Finnish society and take her shoes off indoors. My heart burst. I scooped her up in a bear hug and she clung to me with arms and legs like a spider monkey hanging on to its mother. In my peripheral vision I saw everyone watching us with mouths open in surprise. No one even scolded us about her shoes, because foreigners had special dispensation for not understanding Finnish customs, even if we have lived here for ten years.

There were about a dozen family members and friends in the room, but I was the one Nea was so excited to see. I was always the quiet loner sitting by himself watching others interact, but thanks to Nea I was now the heart of the gathering. But even the pride of being chosen was submerged by pure joy at her reaction. I clung to her like she was my only connection to human society, which in a way she was.

I carried Nea back to the front door so she could take off her shoes and coat. She led me by the hand through the watching crowd to see her room. Niilo was not pleased to see my attention on his sister and a furious competition erupted. I tried to diplomatically give time to each of them, but emotional Nea finally had enough and stomped away.

'Finally! Now the boys can be alone,' Niilo said.

He sighed dramatically, which made me laugh. Niilo opened a box and pulled out his computer, monitor, keyboard and mouse. I sat on the floor to be at his level as he set up his gaming battlestation.

'Your English is really good,' I told Niilo. 'You speak it better than Nea or your Mom.'

'I learn it from Youtube and playing games online.'

'What do you play?'

'Roblox, mainly. I also play Minecraft.'

'I play Minecraft some,' I told him. 'Minttu introduced me to it. We played together in the summer in your old apartment.'

He waved her off as inconsequential when it came to gaming.

'I'll build you something cool in Minecraft. The next time you come you can play it.'

'Thanks. That will be fun.'

Niilo suddenly climbed out from under his desk and threw assorted computer cables on the ground. He looked in one box, couldn't find what he wanted and ran out into the hallway. I thought I had been abandoned and was about to leave when Niilo reappeared.

'Here,' he said. 'I made you something at school.'

It was a small piece of plywood, about 25 centimetres square. The wood was covered by a base coat of white. On the centre-right was a thick red zigzag with sharp angles. On the left was a lighter red crescent of thinner paint. In the centre-left was a messy black oval with deliberate hints of brushstrokes breaking away from its margins. I was struck by it. It gave a faraway rumour of abstract expressionists like Franz Kline.

'Wow, Niilo,' I said. 'Thank you very much. I like it a lot.'

He gave me a hug and disappeared under his desk again like a badger diving into its burrow. I went back to the living room and noticed the others watching me through different lenses, now coloured by Nea's rapturous greeting no one had expected. Yet I ignored all the others studying me. Shy Minttu was hanging back, pensively looking at me from across the room, so I went to give her a hug hello and ask about her new home and what had been going on in her life.

Nea reappeared and demanded her favourite game, which was to be picked up and tossed around. This is the reason I've been working out, I realised. It's so I can wrestle with the kids without getting worn out or straining a muscle.

Nea was affectionate and sometimes just wanted to be held for a tight hug. The group was slowly thinning out, but everyone smiled as they watched us play. When Nea left to help unpack her clothes suddenly Minttu was in front of me, arms out and a smile on her face, wanting to be picked up too.

'Ei,' Kaarle said to her in his disciplinarian voice. 'Et ole liian vanha.'

Minttu's face and arms fell. There was nothing worse for her than to be scolded, and the look on her face sent a sudden pain through my chest. It felt like someone had jabbed an icicle under my ribcage. I reached down and squeezed her knee.

'I'm not ticklish,' she informed me stoically.

'Oh, really?' I tickled her ribs and she squealed with laughter.

With a smile back on her face my heart beat normally again. I went into the kitchen to get a drink of water and say hello to Kaarle's mother Kirsti, who was sitting at the kitchen table. Through the window I saw Kaarle and his brother-in-law go out into the yard and haul some summer tyres into their shed. Minttu ran into the kitchen and slid to a stop in front of me, arms out and an apprehensive but excited smile on her face. I immediately scooped her off her feet and groaned at her weight. She squee'd with delight, which got Kirsti laughing as well.

'You'll never be too old for this, but you are a bit big,' I told her, trusting that Kirsti had not heard Kaarle's prohibition. 'How much do you weigh?'

'I'm ninety kil...pounds.' Her face was split into a giant grin as I held her.

'That sound's right, but I'm surprised you know the imperial measurements. Do they teach them in school?'

'No.'

'You learned them for me, didn't you? You learned pounds and miles and degrees Fahrenheit so you could talk to me.'

'Yes.'

'Aw! That is so sweet,' Kirsti said and I thought.

As I gave her a squeeze I heard Kaarle. He always used a specific tone of voice when he scolded his kids, stressed to show he was serious but controlled and conversational in volume. I put Minttu down on her feet. Kaarle stood in the doorway, glaring at her, angry, surprised and more than a little hurt. Minttu glanced quickly at me and lowered her face.

'I'm sorry, man,' I said. 'I was just playing and picked her up. Don't blame her.'

Relief flashed across his face—of course Minttu hadn't disobeyed him—but then he scowled again when he realised what that meant. Minttu hadn't defied him, but I had.

'It's okay,' he said, choosing to accept my apology and not go any further. 'No problem.'

Kirsti asked something about the new house and Kaarle turned to her. Minttu and I smiled secretly at each other. We had gotten away with it.

'Do you want to play Hit the Hat?' she asked.

'I'm happy to play anything with you,' I told her, 'but you'll have to teach me how.'

Minttu ushered me into her new bedroom and shut the door. She opened a box on the floor and pulled out a board game. Hit the Hat involved a roll of the dice which revealed what type and colour of hat you were supposed to find. A number of cards depicted all the possible combinations, and the goal was to hit a suction-cupped stick on the relevant card before your opponent found it. Minttu had an astonishingly quick eye and collected about three times as many cards as I did as we played.

The door suddenly banged open. Kaarle was in the doorway with a concerned look on his face.

'So here you guys are,' he said. 'You both disappeared and we didn't know where you were.'

'We're playing Hit the Hat,' I said. 'It's fun but I'm not very good.'

He smiled at me and turned to Minttu. 'The TV's hooked up and our show is starting. Do you want to come watch?'

'I want to play with David.'

Kaarle hesitated, chewing his lip and looking at me like he had something else to say, but he nodded and left. He had left the door open but as soon as Niilo appeared in the doorway Minttu yelled 'Ulos, ulos!' and shut the door on him.

'What's your television show?' I asked her.

'NCIS. We watch it together every night.'

Minttu spoke casually, unconcerned, but Kaarle had been bothered. She was not his biological daughter, but they were close in ways I would never understand. He had named his boat after her, which for him was a more definitive statement of his feelings than getting a tattoo of her name. Yet now she had nonchalantly dismissed a father-daughter custom to play a game with me.

Minttu and I played several more games of Hit the Hat. I only won one, and I suspected that was due to her letting me win. Later we changed to a different game, where we used little plastic fishing rods to catch animatronic fish which opened and closed their mouths. Minttu was good at this, too.

'You have a delicate and precise touch,' I told her. 'Maybe you will grow up to be a surgeon.'

'Maybe,' Minttu said. 'But I like coding. I might be a programmer.'

The door opened again, this time more calmly. Kaarle came in Minttu's bedroom and sat down on a big rubber yoga ball. I was glad to see him smiling as he watched us play. He was wearing his coat.

'Is that coat for me?' I asked. 'Are you subtly telling me that you're ready to take me home?'

'Whenever you're ready.'

'I had a lot of fun, kulta,' I told Minttu, giving her a hug. 'Send me a message about what you think about your new home.'

Nea was eager to show me a few things in her new room, but Kaarle waited patiently until I could say goodbye to her and Niilo and extricate myself. All the other helpers had already gone, and Kaarle and I walked out into the dark, silent yard lit by their porch light and jumped into Fucker. About halfway through the long drive to Lauttasaari Kaarle suddenly said: 'The girls love you.'

His voice was complex, half-amused and half-accusatory, and I had to think how to respond.

'I like them, too,' I said carefully. 'But I'm new and exotic. They'll lose interest when my novelty wears off.'

In the darkness of the car I felt Kaarle's head turn to look at me, but he did not speak.

14

The only visitors I had had since I moved in was the Jehovah's Witnesses, so when I heard a knock on the door I figured they had come back to save my soul. At least someone was trying. But no, it was two guys from the building management company which handled my block of flats.

'There was a leak a couple of floors above you, so we need to check if you have any damage,' one said in English, forewarned by my name that I was a foreigner. His companion nodded and smiled blankly at me, a sure sign he didn't speak English.

'Come in, come in,' I said. 'I haven't noticed anything.'

Both were thirty-something with dark hair and dark work clothes. The non-English speaker had glasses and carried a clipboard with a thick bunch of paper on it, with about half flipped over and held to the back by grubby fingers. The English speaker had a small flashlight which he handled as if it was an extension from his hand. They didn't bother to take off their shoes.

I followed them as they checked the point where the ceiling met the wall in my bathroom, kitchen and main room. The English speaker quickly flashed the light at an area and moved on to the next. It took approximately ten seconds.

'No water damage!' he said, 'But what happened here?' He gestured to a giant gouge on the drywall close to the door.

'I have no idea. It was here when I moved in.'

They conferred in low Finnish voices and the other glanced at a couple of the pages on his clipboard, shaking his head.

'It is not on the…' he searched for a word, 'form you fill out when you move in.'

'What form?'

'You received a form with other materials about the apartment when you moved in.'

I opened up the closet and pulled out a thick binder about the flat. Most of the material were user manuals of various appliances, along with a few sheets regarding the dimensions and history of my flat. In the front pocket were several papers, one of which he pointed at. It looked to be a checklist with a number of mysterious words like lattia, jääkaappi and uuni.

'That one,' he said. 'You were supposed to report any damages you found when you moved in. Now you are responsible for that damage.'

I closed the binder.

'Ah, the foreigner tax,' I said.

'Mitä?'

'It's the extra costs all foreigners have to pay in Finland. They don't have networks to tell them how things work. Foreigners can't ask old friends because they don't have any. They can't get their family to help because they are alone. They don't understand the contracts they have to sign so end up paying more than they expected. They don't know about consumer protection laws so get ripped off.'

'That's not our fault you don't understand things,' he said. 'You signed the contract. You chose to come here, so learn our language.'

They left, talking loudly in Finnish and slamming my door.

Well, he isn't wrong, I thought.

15

Fucking Finnish. I hate it. The Finnish language is the result of a thousand generations of people living and dying in fetid huts, surrounded by fields of mud under corpse-grey skies, grunting and growling at each other as they fingered their notched pukkos in the firelight.

If a Finn were to say such a thing people would laugh, because Finns love self-deprecating humour, but I am not a Finn. When I criticise or ridicule something Finnish Finns close ranks and attack me to protect their own. I am not allowed to say this because I am an outsider, but I did it anyway.

I quietly fumed on my daily walk, or search. I stopped in front of a pole with a series of street signs. I read:

- Ei koski
- linja-autoja
- erityisluvalla

It was meaningless gibberish. I couldn't understand a single word except for 'auto' which I assumed meant 'car'. Ten years in the country had given me a million instances of puzzling over signs, frowning during conversations, Google Translating websites, mispronouncing names. The countless blank smiles, shaking heads, awkward glances away. Anteeksi. En puhu suomea. Anteeksi. En puhu suomea. It was the mantra of my Finnish existence.

I had taken a half dozen Finnish language classes, but Finnish still remained an impenetrable mystery to me. This was hard to accept. I think I am of average intelligence, but I couldn't learn the language like other foreigners manage to do. I had really tried and still failed. Deep down you have an idea that you have immense capability, that if you work hard for something you will achieve it, but this is just a fairy tale told to children to encourage them and insulate them from the harshness of reality. I could blame my age, or my shitty American language education, or any number of things, but those are all lies. I'm not good enough. Not only was my failure hard to take personally, my inability to learn the language kept me from truly calling Finland home. It was impossible to ever integrate into a country when I couldn't speak the language.

But there were more words on the sign.

-Gäller ej
- bussar
- med special-tillstånd

This was Swedish, one of Finland's official languages. Most public notices of this sort were written in both Finnish and Swedish. I could at least pick out a few more words. Bussar must mean busses, so my guess that the line was about passenger cars was wrong. I could read 'special' as well, but this didn't tell me much more. At least I could read two words in Swedish, but the one word in Finnish I thought I knew turned out to be wrong.

Maybe I should focus on Swedish. If I learned Swedish I would be able to speak with Finns, read their books, connect with what is happening in society. No longer would I need people to translate for me, or speak English just for my benefit, or use Google Translate to make an online purchase. Finally I would truly belong.

This sounded good, but nagging doubts remained. Even the Swedish-speakers knew Finnish. I had only heard of rare cases of elderly people in tiny coastal towns who weren't fluent in Finnish.

Everyone spoke Finnish, except maybe in Åland, so how useful would Swedish be in my ordinary life? Perhaps I could do my taxes in Swedish, but my landlord hadn't even offered a Swedish version of the apartment inspection form. Would a sales clerk use it with me, or a waiter, or a receptionist at an office? What about Robert or Kaarle?

Leaving the inscrutable sign behind I continued my walk and continued to think. I had been intrigued when I had learned of Swedish-speaking Finns, back when I first came to Finland. The idea of another language being spoken by a chunk of the population is nothing unusual throughout the world, but it was fascinating to someone from Indiana. Besides Dad praying in Latin I had never even heard someone speak a language other than English until I was in my late teens.

My first job in Finland was in the investment services industry, which seemed to have a disproportionately high number of Swedish speakers. The old joke in finance was you spoke Finnish to your clients, English to your colleagues and Swedish to your boss. I was taking Finnish classes, but a number of my co-workers told me to learn Swedish instead. At my first pikkujoulu, or Little Christmas party, I quizzed one of the salesmen about it. This was also my first experience with discrimination against Swedish speakers.

'Fuck Swedish,' the salesman, Jari, philosophised.

'Fuck Swedish, huh?' asked Nina, the Swedish-speaking back office administrator.

Jari was drunk, but not so drunk as to realise this was a good time to shut his mouth. I didn't understand what was going on, but the tension was thick.

When I went home I asked Heljä about it and discovered that she, too, was not fond of Swedish speakers.

'They're rich snobs,' she had replied.

I tried to judge her comment by my own experience. The Swedish-speakers at work didn't seem snobbish but I had heard

Swedish in the expensive Stockmann grocery store. Rich businessman Björn Wahlroos from Sampo was a Swedish speaker. Hundreds of years ago Swedish was the language of the governing class and gentry. Maybe they were a shadow aristocratic class even today who looked down on Finnish speakers. How would I know?

Eventually I met more Swedish-speaking people and knew them well enough to ask questions. Yes, there is prejudice against us, they told me. Some were angry and bitter about it, and some just shrugged their shoulders. One person took my education a step forward and invited me to a crayfish party in a Swedish-speaking rural area. I was greeted by dozens of people chewing tobacco and wearing work boots and overalls. One even wore a straw hat, which I at first thought was some kind of joke. They were friendly and pleasant and hospitable to me as a stranger, just like practically any rural people you meet anywhere in the world. They would be right at home in southern Indiana.

These people aren't rich snobs, I thought. They're hillbillies. They're small town farmers!

My walk over, I returned to my dark flat and tried to get back to work, but I kept thinking about my communication problems. I should focus on Swedish, I thought. Yet a voice in my mind kept telling me I was choosing Swedish because I was too stupid to learn Finnish. Swedish is so much easier than Finnish for an English speaker. An English speaker could understand many words with no effort at all. You—du. Here—här. Dog—hund. I researched a line from one of my favourite books, *The Hobbit*. I could read the Swedish sentence without much effort, but the Finnish was completely incomprehensible.

'Good morning!' said Bilbo, and he meant it.

'God morgon!' sade Bilbo, och han menade det.

'Hyvät huomenet!' sanoi Bilbo ja tarkoitti mitä sanoi.

Fine. I like Swedish because it is easier for me. So what? It wasn't just the language and people which I liked, but the very concept. Swedish-speaking Finns were outsiders, in a sense, a minority in their own little duck pond. The Swedish-speaking Finns were not a homogenous group, but the language was like a password to get into an exclusive club. I once saw two strangers introduce themselves to each other, and when they realised they were both Swedish speakers their smiles had slightly widened and their handshakes became a bit more animated. Ah! How nice! We're in the same group, they seemed to say. That attracted me, because I was an outsider, too. I wanted someone to say that to me, to recognise me as a member of their community.

But the little voice continued to poke and prod old wounds. Another reason you are attracted to Swedish, it said, is because Heljä hates it.

As our marriage slowly rotted away more and more of our opinions seemed formed solely to oppose each other. This was mostly unconscious, but was the inevitable result when you don't like each other. I had only become a clean freak after living with her messiness. She used to love books but completely rejected literature when I became a professional writer. She liked tomatoes; I hated them. She hated Swedish; I liked it.

I didn't even realise this until after the divorce, when so many of my tastes suddenly changed. I had refused to eat tomatoes for years and now I was having them daily. I had sneered at my ex-wife's beloved Instagram but the simple fact Minttu liked it made me like it, too. Would my enthusiasm for the Swedish language cool without Heljä's hatred to keep it warm? No, I decided. I'm sure it won't. None of her opinions mattered anymore and had no influence over me. In fact, as far as I was concerned she didn't exist. But that little voice wouldn't be silenced.

Yes, she does, it said.

16

My already overburdened time management system reeled when I dedicated myself to learning Swedish. My packed categories of Freelance Writing, Mental Health and Physical Health were now joined by Svenska. I aspirationally decided to list all my tasks in the Swedish category in the Swedish language.

After beginning with online vocabulary builders and a few astonishingly cheap Swedish classes at Arbis I refined my tasks. I kept a diary in Swedish. I watched Swedish news and changed the homepage on my computer from the BBC to Svenska YLE. Every time I took the stairs I mentally counted the steps in Swedish. My shopping lists were in Swedish. I borrowed the print and audio formats of the same book in Swedish from the library. I read along with the speaker and hit pause after each sentence or phrase and repeated out loud what I had just heard, trying to pronounce the unfamiliar sounds correctly.

Yet to learn the language I needed to communicate with it. This was a problem because outside of work I interacted very little with other people. I could spend literally days and not leave my desk, only communicating with clients and editors via phone and email and getting my daily chat with Minttu and Chris on messaging apps. Perhaps I could use Swedish in my work? I was working twelve-hour days, so if I could integrate Swedish into that I could make my time doubly productive.

I compiled a list of Swedish companies in the sectors I specialised in, and found a number of traditionally Swedish-speaking businesses in Finland. My introductory email was re-written, now including clues that I was at least familiar with Swedish. Instead of only mentioning my Nokia book I also included the obviously Swedish name of the publisher. The examples of my articles were all changed to those about Swedish-speaking firms. To top it off, I even changed the greeting of my letter from Hello to Hej and the closing from Sincerely to Hälsningar.

It was the act of a poser, but it worked. I picked up four new clients: a Swedish content agency, a major Swedish tech firm, a Finnish financial services company with roots in the Swedish-speaking population, and a venerable Finnish industrial company owned by a Swedish-speaking family. Three of the new customers only gave me small and irregular jobs, but the Swedish tech firm was soon giving me two or three articles a week. I still wrote everything in English, but now I was getting background information I had to read in Swedish.

My reading and writing were improving—if not quickly at least persistently. But the biggest problem was having conversations. Here my skills were woefully undeveloped. A few tentative attempts to say 'hur mår du?' to some Swedish-speakers I knew brought confused stares. The only way to learn was to do it. I needed to talk to people, face-to-face. I told myself this was in order to learn Swedish, but there were other deeper, more fundamental needs also involved. I was lonely.

Finns are notoriously shy and untalkative. My nature is similar, which makes it difficult to spontaneously start conversations. I memorised about twenty stock Swedish phrases as conversation starters. It was not unusual to hear Swedish on the island where I lived, and I suspected I would be able to find someone to talk to. It was a warm sunny day and I could see people outside through my window. With the Swedish phrases swirling in my head and an absurdly cheerful demeanour I went out to converse in Swedish.

The first person I met was a man in a business suit carrying a briefcase, and I chickened out at the last moment, letting him pass unaccosted. The second person was a woman talking on a phone, who I obviously couldn't speak to. The third was the outsider Widow's Peak, who gave me the Nod as he passed. No, I couldn't speak to one of the other outsiders. That would break our unwritten code.

This wasn't working. I needed to just talk to someone. I promised myself that I would speak to the next person I saw, who happened to be a young boy peddling his bike slowly home from school. I frantically searched through my list of phrases for something suitable.

'Fin cykel!' I said to him as he approached.

He eyed me suspiciously and peddled away without a word. Wait. Did I say 'fin' or 'fan'? I wondered nervously if I had praised or profaned his bike.

What about a store? The people working there have to talk to you. I went into the small shabby grocery store close to the swimming beach and picked up a bottle of water. There were two people in line ahead of me and I nervously rehearsed my line again and again until it was my cue to go on stage.

'Jag gillar dina örhängen!' I blurted to the cashier.

She stared at me and offered the receipt. 'Kuitti,' she mumbled.

No, I wasn't going to give up. On my list of daily tasks was to have one conversation in Swedish, and by God, I was going to have one conversation in Swedish before I went back to work.

As I walked down the sidewalk a woman came into view. She was about thirty, blond, alone, and she was walking a little fluffy dog which was already pulling on the leash to get to me, desperate to say hello.

'Jag gillar din hund,' I said, without much hope.

She brightly responded with a slurred machine gun of sounds. I didn't recognise a single syllable, much less any meaning. I gave up.

'Sorry,' I switched to English and knelt down to play with the dog. 'I'm just learning Swedish and didn't understand.'

'I said she likes you too.'

'I brought a dog with me from America but he died about two years ago. I really miss him.'

'Have you ever thought about getting a new dog?'

'Maybe someday,' I said, still on my knees with the dog.

'Or you could walk someone else's dog. I used to do that before I got my own.'

'Can I walk your dog?'

She laughed. 'You can walk with us. Do you want to come with us now?'

I looked at my watch.

'I would, but I need to call a client in fifteen minutes.'

'I can call you the next time we go out.'

'Great! Here. My number is on my card.'

Within ten minutes she had sent me her number, and in the evening she sent another message asking if I wanted to go for a walk with her and her dog. She signed it 'Saga,' which was how I learned her name. I was in the middle of washing dishes but abandoned them to soak in the gunmetal sink and went out to meet her.

Previously my wandering had mostly been confined to the edges of the island because the sea drew me. Saga had grown up deep in the interior of Finland, Jyväskylä, and had been pulled to the inner ways of Drumsö, the Swedish name of Lauttasaari. She introduced me to little parks, streets and neighbourhoods inland which I hadn't known had existed.

After about an hour and a half of wandering we stopped in front of my building. I tried to go in, but she remained standing and chatting about something or other.

'Would you like to come up?' I asked, uncharacteristically getting the hint.

'Sure.'

We walked up to my flat and I let her in. We took off our shoes in the cramped hallway. Saga looked into the bathroom for several seconds and moved to the kitchen.

'You said you like to bake, but you can't bake in here,' she announced.

'I put the coffee machine on the floor, and I can also open up the cutting-board drawer and use that for more space. It's tight, but you can do it.'

She walked into the main room and studied my bed.

'What the hell is this?'

'I had an incident ordering a new bed.'

'It is as high as my chest. It looks like you have two

mattresses.'

'I do have two mattresses. I didn't understand what I was ordering. Everything was in Finnish.'

'You should have asked for help.'

I shrugged. 'I need to learn how to survive here without constantly asking someone to help me. When I mess up I need to live with the consequences.'

Saga hopped up on my bed, with a franticly happy dog standing up to scratch at her dangling feet.

'This is such a bachelor pad,' she laughed suddenly. 'You just need a poster of a half-naked woman on the wall.'

'Good idea. Maybe a Candace Swanepoel. I have a thing for her.'

'That Victoria's Secret model? She's hot.' Saga nodded approvingly. 'Where do you work?'

'Right there at that desk. I'm a writer.'

'Like what? Books?'

'Yes, and articles.'

'Anything I would know?'

'My last book was about Nokia.'

She cocked her head and looked at me, thinking for a moment.

'What was it called?'

'*The Decline and Fall of Nokia.*'

'I've heard of that.'

I didn't answer and sat on the floor. Saga's dog immediately ran to me, yipping with excitement. Suddenly Saga let out a laugh.

'You don't even have a table!'

'Nowhere to put one.'

'Then I guess we'll hang out at my place.'

17

The next night Saga invited me over to her flat to bake a lemon cake recipe she wanted to try. After ten minutes of continually brushing past each other in the kitchen our jeans were around our ankles and she was bent over the counter. I discovered she had nipple piercings, which flicked a turbo switch in my primitive brain which had been almost completely dormant during my marriage.

When Saga went into the bathroom I seated myself at her kitchen table and surreptitiously looked at an envelope from her bank, which was how I learned her last name.

'Come on,' she said. 'This cake isn't going to bake itself.'

We returned to the counter where all the ingredients had been scattered and abandoned.

'I was going to ask you to bring vanilla sugar with you when you came, but you didn't answer your messages,' Saga said.

'I was busy, and I turn off my phone when I'm busy. I had three guys to interview today.'

'"Guys",' she quoted. 'Don't you ever interview women?'

'Yeah, sometimes. But normally I don't pick who to interview. That is done by the clients.'

'But what about the writing you do control, like your books?'

'Well, the biography was about a man and most of the Nokia executives were men as well,' I said. 'But in my novel one of the main characters is a woman.'

'Who is she?'

'The mistress of the Roman Emperor. She...'

'Oh, for fuck's sake. She is even defined by her role as a sexual outlet to a man.'

I opened my mouth to snap back at her but stopped. Damn, I thought, she's right. I never thought of it like that before.

Lemon cake forgotten, Saga stared at me.

'Have you ever considered that you're a bit misogynistic in your work?' she asked.

'I hope I'm not misogynistic,' I said. 'When it comes to the articles, I write a lot about technology and there are few females in that field that my clients want interviewed. I can't control that.

With my books I try to write things from my point of view and I'm a man. There are women writers who can speak for the feminist point of view much better than I ever could.'

'Like who? Have you ever read a feminist author?'

'Margaret Atwood is a genius. Here in Finland one of my favourites is Maria Turtschaninoff.'

'I know about Turtschaninoff. She writes fantasy for girls, right?'

'I don't know if they are *for* girls necessarily, but the main characters are female. In one book there is a character who identifies as a woman and I didn't even notice that it was a he until it got another character pregnant.'

'*She*!' Saga shouted. 'She isn't a fucking "it". If she wants to be called a woman she is a woman. It is a human right for every individual to define, or refuse to define, their own gender identity. This bullshit patriarchy misgendering is oppression.'

'Okay, okay. I meant "it" as a character, not as a person. Listen, I'm not trying to be offensive.'

'No, now you're defensive.'

'Maybe I am, but I have a right to be. Saga, you can't get angry at me because I don't know this stuff. My only experience is a girl I know who is in a relationship with a person who looks very much like a girl but uses a male name and wants to be called a "he". And that's fine with me. I don't care. It's only polite to address a person the way they want to be addressed.'

'FTM,' she noted.

'I don't understand what you are talking about.'

'Female To Male. He was assigned female at birth but identifies as male. Why haven't you talked to him about it?'

'We're not close. He's dating my ex's half-sister. I'm not comfortable just blurting out personal questions like this.'

'You should ask. If you do it politely and respectfully—and cut out the microaggressions—he won't take offense.'

'Well, I'm asking you. Instead of yelling at me when I

innocently make a mistake you could just tell me what is appropriate. I'm not afraid of learning.'

Saga smiled.

'Okay,' she said. 'It's a deal.'

18

Saga thought it was cute that I took notes.

'I'm a writer,' I explained. 'I think best with a pen in my hand.'

My notes were a confused mess, just like my notes were when I began to study Swedish. In many ways this comparison was apt because the LGBTQIA community (Lesbian, Gay, Bisexual, Transgender, Queer / Questioning, Intersex, Asexual, my notes read) had their own vocabulary. Cisgender, dysphoria, gender-fluid, bears and ursulas, binary, male to female, monosexism, pansexual, transmisogyny, tomboi, queer…

'It's interesting how the community has reclaimed the word "queer" and made it their own,' I said. 'It is the same as what the African-American community did with the n-word.'

'You said "queer" but not "nigger",' Saga noted. 'That's interesting.'

'It's a tough word for Americans. Neekeri is still used so casually among Finns that many don't understand why Americans are so uncomfortable with it. It has a long and dark history in American society which makes it difficult to explain. It is like saying Finland is cold. The cold doesn't just mean you need proper clothes when you go outside. There is so much more to the story. Finland's cold defines the agriculture, the power grid, art, language, sports—it just goes on and on. The word nigger is the same way. It doesn't just mean an insult. It has deep roots through the whole of American history, economics and society.'

'There! Now you know what it feels like when you use sexual or gender terms incorrectly.'

Saga was tired of teaching, and I was tired of constantly

watching my terminology, so we consoled each other with a hug which quickly evolved. I couldn't keep my hands away from her barbell nipple rings as we moved to the bedroom.

As the events progressed she asked me to first slap and then to choke her. Initially I did it hesitatingly, like I was scolding a kitten, but she ordered that I be serious about it, so I was. Afterwards I lay on her bed and wondered about the feelings that brought up in me, and what feelings came up in her, and how that related to her feminism, but before I could even begin to guess Saga called me back to myself.

'I bought some blueberries today,' she said. 'Let's make a pie.'

'Goddamn you switch topics fast.'

'No need to dwell on things. Focus on the present, not the past.'

She wanted a Finnish-style pie, which was quite a bit different from the fruit pies of America. American pies tended to use contrasts with a salty crust and sweet filling. Finnish pies used complementary tastes like a sweet crust and a crème fraiche filling which was almost cakelike. I was beginning to prefer Finnish pies but still liked to make American ones on occasion. We put the pie in the oven and Saga set an old-school kitchen timer. It ticked contentedly in the background.

'Let's go out on the balcony,' she said. Her cheekbones were still red from my slaps.

I sat on her balcony loveseat and she appeared a minute later with a stained-glass pipe, a crumpled paper baggie and a lighter. She filled the pipe, held the lighter over the edge of the bowl as she inhaled and passed both speculatively to me. I accepted and took a tentative inhalation.

'Wait,' I said in a puff of smoke. 'We need something for this.'

I handed back the pipe and lighter, walked inside her flat and went to her computer. I returned to the balcony accompanied by *Sgt. Pepper's Lonely Hearts Club Band* blaring from her speakers.

'Of course you put that on,' Saga laughed. 'That is so you.'

The marijuana affected me slowly, thoroughly. It was Stoicism in smoke. Everything was cool; nothing mattered. I felt so satisfied. The money problems were gone, I hardly ever thought about the divorce, I was developing new and meaningful relationships, a blueberry pie was baking, I had that after-sex glow, and the greatest band of all time was playing on the speakers. I was cruising on mellow bliss.

I sang along to the next song, *With a Little Help from My Friends*, only stopping when she handed me the pipe for my turn. There was a tiny jagged piece in the carb hole—one imperfection—which I couldn't stop feeling with my finger. Saga grinned at me, amused, patronising, as I sang along with my horrible voice to the fifty-year-old record. But suddenly during *Lucy in the Sky with Diamonds* Saga exuberantly joined in the chorus.

'Lucy in the sky with diamonds!

Lucy in the sky with diamonds!'

We yelled the lyrics in delight, our voices quivering in that blurry line between singing and shouting. A man walked by on the sidewalk below, glancing up curiously. We didn't care. He didn't exist. Nothing existed except for this instant. Right here, right now, I thought with a pure and sober clarity. You are happy again. It's so rare, so unusual. Remember this moment until the darkness falls.

Because you know it will.

19

Saga soon learned about my idiosyncrasies. My phone was offline from nine am to seven pm. Even when it was online all notifications were disabled. I was working, as the cliché goes, and must not be disturbed. She tried to contact me a few times in the afternoon, asking me to come over, and I didn't see her messages until later in the evening. Saga rescinded her invitations when I replied, perhaps as punishment for not immediately responding, or maybe because she had lost interest and found something else to do.

She eventually learned that I was only available in the evenings and weekends. When I finished my work I contacted her to ask if she wanted to do something. Often, but not always, she said yes and I walked the kilometre to her flat. Sometimes she wasn't in the mood so I read Philip Roth and Tove Jansson and Fyodor Dostoevsky and fell asleep. When I did go to her flat we often baked. Saga tended towards cakes and pies while I was more inclined to make pastries and breads. She was impressed that I took the time and effort to make traditional Finnish ryebread using sourdough, and I was baffled how her unconventional recipes turned out so wonderful. We laughed, we argued, she taught me about social justice, I couldn't keep my hands off of the barbell piercings in her nipples.

Sometimes Saga would produce pill bottles. They had unpronounceable names on them and had originally come from Estonian pharmacies. Sometimes the bottles were brand new and sometimes they looked like they had been handled for years. She occasionally took the ferry to Tallinn with two friends—Tiina and Jussi, who also happened to be her ex-boyfriend—and returned with pill bottles.

I loved Oxycontin. My body felt like I had just had a two-hour sauna followed by a deep tissue massage. All the stress just melted from my muscles. And I was so blissful. Late-paying clients and impossible deadlines dissolved away in the face of my unperturbability. We swallowed Oxycontin and smiled laboratory-induced artificial smiles in the dying sun, our faces bathed in blood light.

20

As I made my morning inspection of what social media's algorithms wanted me to see I came across a post from Mari on Facebook. I struggled to make sense of it. The more Swedish I learned the less

Finnish I understood. I painfully made out that my godson Niilo was going to the children's clinic for some procedure. Niilo had had stomach problems for a long time, and I knew Kaarle and Mari had talked to a doctor about it, so I figured they were going to check him out. That's good, I thought abstractly, hopefully they can help.

I went back to my life, my job, my writing, and didn't give it another thought. Two days later I looked at Facebook and found another post from Mari.

'Taas mennään, tosin hieman aikataulusta jäljessä,' she had posted. 'Aamulla kun oli ylimääräisiä hommia, onneksi Minsu hoitaa loput tehtävät, niin Niilon ei tarvitse odotella kauheasti.'

She was going back, but behind schedule. In the morning there was something-or-other, but someone—who was Minsu?—took care of it. Luckily Niilo doesn't have to wait too long.

What was she talking about? Going back where? The hospital? It sounded like Niilo was waiting there, but this was two days after their appointment. Surely he wasn't still at the hospital, I thought.

I sent a message to Kaarle, saying that I knew Niilo had had some doctor's appointment and asked how he was doing.

Kaarle replied with a picture of Niilo as his usual cheerful self. He was wearing a red foam nose and making a face at the camera. Yet he was lying in a hospital bed, clad in hospital scrubs, with the shirt tied up in a knot to reveal a stomach covered with tubes and surgical tape. It looked like they had put Niilo back together after an encounter with Jack the Ripper.

'He had a surgery,' Kaarle wrote. 'That should fix the problem.'

I was flabbergasted. This wasn't a doctor's appointment. This was a major operation. It looked like they had given Niilo a colostomy.

'Is he home now?' I sent Kaarle.

'In hospital, been since Wednesday and probably have to be there at least one more day.'

I was floored. My little buddy Niilo had been in the hospital for days as I bumbled around my daily routine, completely clueless.

'Tell him I said hello and I'm thinking of him,' I wrote. 'And if you guys need anything let me know.'

It was so trite. So bullshit. My godson was recovering in a hospital and I had done nothing. I hadn't been to see him, or sent flowers, or even thought about him. My friends had a major event in their family, and I hadn't said a word. I hadn't offered to feed their dogs or watch their kids or pick up their mail or anything. They probably thought I was a terrible person. I didn't know! I wanted to explain. I can't understand the fucking language!

The next day Mari had a new post. 'Jee, Niilo pääsee tänään kotiin.'

Yay, Niilo something today to home. Google Translate was little help, but apparently he was coming home today. I wallowed in my regret and shame for a couple of more days and messaged Kaarle again.

'How is Nilo doing? I still feel bad I didn't come to see him in the hospital.'

I looked at the message I had sent and realised that I had fucked up again. If they wanted confirmation that I didn't give a shit about him, misspelling his name was a good way to do it.

'*Niilo,' I added, and then appended another postscript in a weak attempt at justification: 'Damn Finnish language.'

Kaarle replied: 'Don't worry about that. Niilo is much better now. He is getting back to school next week.'

But I did worry about it. My inability to understand Finnish was harming my relationships. I hadn't visited my godson when he was in hospital because I didn't understand what was going on. Hell, I couldn't even get their names right. Was it Kaarle or Karl? Niilo or Nilo? Who was that Minsu Mari had mentioned? It must be a nickname, but I was in the dark as to whose. Names were such a fundamental part of who we are, how we see ourselves. If someone gets your name wrong you remember it. It is an insult, like you don't care enough to know the person.

Well, maybe I don't, I thought. Maybe deep down I don't care about them. Perhaps in reality I'm just using them.

21

I should have simply told Kaarle and Mari that I felt guilty and wanted to see Niilo and play with their kids. That was the easiest and most truthful thing to do, but I was hesitant to open up like that. I wasn't the kids' relative; I was just some person who knew their parents. It wasn't appropriate to want to spend time with them. However, if I happened to be visiting and the kids wanted to play with me then that was an entirely different matter. Then it would be socially acceptable to play with them. My reasoning was logical, if built on rickety foundations, so I concocted a cover story.

'Would Mari be willing to take some photos of me?' I messaged Kaarle. 'I need new pictures taken for my website and stuff. All my professional photos were taken when I had short hair. Now I look like an aging rockstar from some band you can't quite remember the name of.'

'LOL!' Kaarle messaged back. 'Sure. Why don't you take the bus here Saturday morning? We are going to Itäkeskus later in the day to get Minttu a dress for her school dance, so when we're done we can drop you off there.'

The nearest bus stop was about ten kilometres away from their house, so Kaarle drove out and picked me up. When we got back to their place we stood in the driveway as I marvelled at everything they had done.

'You've been doing a lot of work around here,' I said. 'Now you have a trampoline, swimming pool, and I see you took down a couple of trees.'

'We're going to clean out that area over the hill, too.'

Minttu opened the door and stood watching. I waved at her and turned back to Kaarle.

'Why's that? You have some nice raspberry bushes there.'

'We're going to plant a little gard…'

'Come *here*, David!' Minttu called plaintively, and I abandoned Kaarle in the middle of his sentence to go to her.

Minttu and I hugged. She was tall enough now that her arms went around my neck instead of around my torso. Niilo and Nea were waiting inside, but I had to fight my way through the slobbering monster dogs to get to them. The fluffy little puppies had turned into miniature ponies. The kids were as delighted to see me as I was to see them, and this made me even happier.

'Niilo, I'm sorry I didn't come and see you. You know how bad my Finnish is, and I didn't understand you were in the hospital,' I said. 'Can I see your stomach?'

He jerked up his shirt. The stoma looked gigantic on his little torso, with a plastic piece held in place by surgical tape.

'That's okay,' he said. 'It doesn't hurt.'

He poked it with a finger, making me wince.

Niilo didn't appear to be concerned about my absence and I was struggling to explain that it bothered me, at least. But before I could figure out how to articulate it Kaarle called us into the kitchen for lunch.

Kaarle, Mari, Minttu, Nea, Niilo and I gathered in their kitchen. A meal at Kaarle and Mari's was an intimate social event. No phones, no television. The entire family sat down at the table together and actually talked to each other. It reminded me of Sunday dinners when I was growing up, the rare times when my entire family had gathered together. It was a huge contrast to my current life. Except on the rare occasions I ate with Saga, I spent all of my meals alone with a plate balanced on my lap.

They had a massive bowl of some pasta dish, with tossed salad and potato salad and those Finnish butter-eye buns for dessert which I liked so well. The younger kids fought over who got to sit next to me, and the older girls showed no sympathy to their recuperating little brother and exerted their authority. Minttu was on my right and Nea was on my left. I interrupted the chatter of mysterious Finnish words and called for everyone's attention.

'Okay,' I said to the group. 'You know I'm a foreigner and I have trouble with the Finnish language and Finnish names. Let's talk about nicknames. I hear people saying Minsu, and I saw Mari write it on Facebook. Who is that?'

Nea burst into laughter, followed by laughs from the others.

Kaarle intervened: 'Minsu is Minttu.'

Okay, that made sense.

'Then you must be Nipa,' I said to Nea.

The laughter was twice as loud this time.

'Nipa is Niilo,' Kaarle said when it died down.

I never would have guessed that. I thought the 'a' sound at the end of a name was feminine.

'Then who is Malla?' I asked.

'Mari,' Kaarle said.

Well, hell. Here the 'a' sound did go with a feminine name. This made no sense to me.

'Nea?' I asked.

'It could be Nensu, I guess, but we normally just say Nea. And I'm Kalle.'

'You're shitting me. I honestly thought Kalle was a completely different name, not a nickname. When someone said Kalle I always thought they were talking about some cousin or uncle,' I said. 'I know this sounds stupid, but Finnish names are really difficult for me, and I want to get them right.'

I held up my finger. Everyone watched expectantly, eyes wide and food forgotten. The idea that someone could not understand their nicknames was a completely new concept to them. Kaarle knew me best, but even he was surprised at the depths of my ignorance. I went around the table, pointing as I went and sometimes hesitating as I tried to remember.

'Minttu is Minsu, Mari is Malla, Niilo is Nipa…and of course Kaale and Nea.'

'Hyvää!' Mari said, nodding approvingly at me and using the same tone of voice as when their dogs sat on command.

I tried to use the nicknames during the remainder of my visit, but I was constantly stumbling over them and trying to remember them by a logical progression.

'What online game are you playing now…' Let's see, his name is Niilo so it must be Nipa… 'Nipa?' I ended lamely.

The names simply didn't make sense to me. 'Danny' was a perfect diminutive for 'Daniel'. But 'Nipa' for 'Niilo'? It was alien. Faltering over the names was making me uncomfortable, and the others weren't enthusiastic at me constantly hesitating and struggling about who they were. It may have been funny the first time, but by the third or fourth it had lost its charm and was verging on the offensive. The only nicknames I had used previously were for the two girls. Nea, who struggled with English, was 'sweetie' while Minttu was the Finnish equivalent 'kulta'. This seemed natural and we were all used to it, so I quietly abandoned my attempt to use Finnish-style nicknames and be like them.

There was already a curtain drawn between us, but this just made it more visible. Names have power. Some Jews refuse to pronounce the name of God. In other sects there is a belief that calling the name of a demon will cause it to appear. It is the same in modern society. Names have a power beyond simple identification. When Kaarle and his family called each other by their nicknames I was excluded, not a member of their tribe, not a user of those sacred names. This episode and my new bit of knowledge was not necessarily beneficial. It just served to remind us how large a gulf there was between us.

22

'Do you want to play piiloleikki?' Nea asked in that slow, careful way in which she used English.

'What's that?'

She frowned, searching for the words, but Minttu helped her out.

'One person counts and the other people hide,' Minttu said.

'You try to find them.'

'That's called hide-and-seek in English. Of course I'll play.'

Kaarle and Mari had the perfect place for hide-and-seek. Their house was surrounded by a large yard, peppered with outbuildings and huge rock outcrops. The house and yard were on the top of a hill which fell away on all sides into a small birch and pine forest filled with bushes and crags and crannies. No one would ever find you if you were serious about hiding.

As the girls debated who would count first I saw Niilo pull up his shirt and try to reattach the tape holding his stoma cap. The tape was losing its adhesive and wasn't sticking to his skin.

'Do you need some more tape?'

'No, it's fine,' Niilo said, but he immediately pulled up his shirt and tried to make it stick again.

'I'll go ask your Mom for more tape.'

'No, it's *okay*,' Niilo stressed.

I was already walking back to the house but turned around to look at him. He pulled off the tape, balled it up and threw it up on the deck.

'I don't need it,' he explained.

Don't make a big deal out of it, I told myself. He knows what he needs. Don't draw attention to it. Treat him just like any other little boy.

As I talked to Niilo his evil sisters conspired to make him to count first. The girls and I scattered. Nea hid behind the tool shed, Minttu disappeared in the wood pile and I crouched behind a large boulder to watch Niilo search for us. Shrieks of laughter in the distance told me when Niilo had found Nea so I snuck over and hid with Minttu. We tried to make each other laugh so Niilo could find us. I was having so much fun I wondered why the smiling Mari had come out into the yard with her camera, before I remembered that I was there to have some pictures taken.

Mari was fast and efficient with her photography, and we followed her inside to look at the pictures on her computer. I picked out a few I wanted.

'USB,' Mari said, waving me down the hallway. 'Minttun huone.'

After a few blank moments I realised she was telling me to get a USB flash drive from Minttu's room so she could save the photos for me. Minttu's bedroom was tiny—actually a converted walk-in closet—but she kept it neat and I immediately spotted the flash drive on her desk. I picked it up and stopped. Next to her computer, in the middle of a tidy stack of papers, was my Nokia book with a bookmark about a third of the way through.

Why in the world would a twelve-year-old girl be reading a business book about Nokia? Minttu was young enough she had probably never even used a Nokia phone. Maybe she was practicing her English, but she could certainly find something more interesting for her. Minttu was attracted to natural sciences like mathematics and biology instead of economics. I stared at the book and had a Eureka moment. No, I had it all wrong. She didn't care at all about the content; she cared about the author. She was reading it because I wrote it.

When I returned to the living room I immediately motioned for Minttu to come to me for a hug. She ran and squeezed me tight. I didn't give a reason for my wanting a hug and she didn't ask for one.

With the photos on the memory stick Mari opened up some new pages on the computer. Minttu needed to pick out new shoes to go with her new dress for the dance. I looked over Mari's left shoulder as Minttu looked over her right. They decided upon a pair of pink shoes with about three-inch stiletto heels.

'Hän ei tarvitse korkokenkiä!' said Kaarle angrily.

'Söpö! Isä ei halua hänen pikkutytön kasvavan aikuiseksi!' Mari said, and jumped up and gave him a hug.

Kaarle's face was pained and slightly embarrassed that the real reason for his objection was so obvious. It was hard for him to accept that his little girl was growing up. She was twelve years' old but looked older. Minttu watched him, her face a tapestry of emotions. She was excited and happy to dress up and dance with boys like a grown-up but was sad because her father was sad. I smiled at Kaarle's silly nostalgic weakness and quietly excused myself to go back outside.

Nea was walking along the handrail of their terrace, her arms stretched out for balance and her tongue out in concentration. My heart kicked a few ribs out of place.

'Nea, come down from there!' I said, hurrying over.

She glanced at me. 'No.'

It was a minor jump down to the wooden deck, but almost a two-metre fall to the ground, where a number of basketball-sized stones circled the deck.

'Let's go inside and play Minecraft!'

'No.'

This time she didn't even look at me. She continued to carefully and slowly walk along the railing. When she reached a lamp mounted on the corner she turned around and lost her balance. It took her a moment, thin little arms windmilling, before she steadied herself.

I knew I should make her obey. For one, it was dangerous what she was doing. Also, I had the vague idea she had to learn to listen to me. You were supposed to set boundaries with kids, or something like that. She had to respect me as an authority figure.

But Kaarle and Mari had never asked me to babysit their kids. They never said that I was in charge or told Nea to listen to me. Also, for all I knew, they were perfectly fine with her walking on the handrail. I had done much more dangerous things when I was Nea's age, and Dad had only watched and laughed. Maybe this wasn't anything to worry about.

She turned again and her foot slipped. I gasped, but she squatted down to steady herself on the rail. Balance restored, she stood up and started walking down the rail again.

This was too much. I thought it was dangerous, and as an

adult mine was the only opinion that mattered right now. What if she fell and broke a leg? I imagined her twisted on the rocks, in pain, in tears, and knowing that it was my fault. Kaarle would be furious. I saw him screaming at me: how could you have let her do that? Don't you have any common sense? You're never going to see my kids again!

I still didn't want to yell at her, to force her to get down. I have always been such a coward for confrontations. So I did what I always did: a weak middle way. I reached up and took Nea's hand to help steady her and to catch her if she fell. This way, I decided, I could protect her without fighting with her. She gave me a smile, her smooth little fingers grabbing tight. She liked holding my hand, so she let me do it.

23

Nea and I were jumping on the trampoline when Mari's parents arrived. They would babysit while the rest of us went to Itäkeskus. It was time to get Minttu's new dress at the shopping mall and drop me off at the bus station. Nea wanted to come too, which caused a brief argument between her and her sister. Eventually Minttu sat in the middle of the back seat with a pouting Nea on her right and an empty seat on the left for me. I hadn't understood what they were saying so wasn't aware that it had been a power struggle regarding who sat next to me. I would have offered to sit in the middle if I had known what the commotion was about, but it was too late now.

About halfway to the mall Nea asked her parents something The only words I recognised were 'David' and 'mukaan'. I forced the tired codebreaker neurons in my brain into work. Mukaan was a preposition of some sort, I thought. With David? By David? As I despairingly pondered what she meant Kaarle looked over at Mari, who smiled and nodded.

'Nea is asking if she can go shopping with you in the mall while we get Minttu's new dress,' Kaarle said.

'Why, certainly. That will be fun!'

Nea beamed, but Minttu's smile disappeared and she stared straight ahead. Her face became stone whenever something bothered her. I playfully poked her ribs, trying to cheer her up.

'I'm not ticklish,' she intoned dryly.

'Yes, you are,' I told her, 'and I know where.'

I squeezed her knee, which rewarded me with a squeal and laugh. I kept tickling as she tried to knock my hands away, until I was certain the smile was back on her face.

'Send me a picture of the dress you are getting,' I said. 'I want to see it.'

'I have one.' Minttu produced her phone and showed me a picture of a pretty pink dress. 'It's for the school dance.'

'No, silly. I don't care about the dress. I meant that I want to see a picture of you wearing it,' I said, and dropped my voice to whisper in her ear: 'Make sure you are wearing your new shoes, too. I thought they looked great.'

Now it was Minttu's turn to beam. She was still smiling when Kaarle parked in the cavernous concrete parking garage at the Itis mall. They weren't going into the mall, at least at first, but were walking down the street to Minttu's dress store. On the verge of being alone in charge of ten-year-old Nea I started to get nervous and peppered Kaarle with questions. When did he want her back? Where should we meet? Was there anything I should know? Is she deathly allergic to anything?

'No, no, it's all cool,' he said, laughing and waving his hand reassuringly. 'We'll be around all afternoon, so whenever you guys are done just call me. And don't let her out of your sight.'

Kaarle gave a mock-stern finger shake at Nea, who grinned and gave him and Mari a hug goodbye. They walked away, leaving me alone with her. I had handled Minttu fine enough by myself, back when they went on holiday and I watched their flat, but Minttu was older, more mature and responsible, and she was already fluent in English. Nea's English was about as good as my

Finnish, meaning it was hideous. But before I could sort through my worries Nea dragged me into the mall.

She darted into the first clothes store we came to and went straight to the little girls' section. Nea is extremely emotive and expressive, unlike everyone else in her family. I could read her face easily, so when she had the cutest abstracted look on her face as she studied a skirt I knew she was considering it.

'Go try it on,' I urged, pointing to a 'sovitus' sign which I expected meant 'changing room' or something similar.

She went into the changing area and I posted myself like a palace guard outside her stall. A few women in the area eyed me suspiciously, but I didn't care. I was going to stick close to Nea whether they liked it or not. Nea tried on the skirt and came out to show it off. She gave a twirl, grinning hugely.

'I like it!' I said, giving her a thumb up.

When she came back out of the stall her face was abstracted again, but now punctuated by frown lines.

'Do you like it?'

'Yes, I like.'

'Do you want it?'

She hesitated.

'I'll buy it if you want it,' I said, gesturing to myself.

'Really? Kiitos!'

I got a hug for my suggestion and another at the cash register. Nea took the bag from the cashier but I stopped her.

'When you go shopping with a man he is supposed to carry the bags,' I explained. 'It is the man's job. We are your Sherpas.'

Nea was in the dark as to what I was saying, but could understand from my body language that I was offering to carry her skirt. She handed it to me.

'Wait,' I suddenly said, thinking of what Saga had taught me. 'No, I was wrong. You have every right to carry the bag if you want. I shouldn't force us into the old, stereotypical gender roles. You see, the woman can carry the bags if she wants...you can wear blue instead of pink if you want, and you can play with trucks instead of dolls, and I have no right to tell you not to carry the bags because...because...'

She stared at me open-mouthed. Nea was the girliest girl who ever girled. She loved Disney princesses and ponies and frilly dresses and glitter and pretty much every stereotypical feminine thing you could imagine. She even had tiaras, for fuck's sake. If she could have understood me she would have been flabbergasted, if not outraged, but she barely spoke English and only caught one word in twenty of what I was saying.

'Never mind,' I said. 'Lead on.'

She shook her head at my craziness and we returned to shopping, me still carrying the bag. My understanding of little girls was academic at best, but I knew they were voracious. Nea claimed she wasn't hungry but when we came to the food court she stopped to stare fixedly at a giant poster of a hamburger. We went in.

We sat at a booth and a waitress arrived. I had to slowly tell Nea to order whatever she wanted several times before she understood what I was saying. Nea ordered in Finnish; I ordered in English; the waitress frowned. She retreated behind the counter to whisper to her colleague. Both stared hard at me. Some foreign man has a little Finnish girl in the restaurant, the women were saying. Something isn't right.

I tried to ignore them and hoped they wouldn't call the cops about a potential abduction. My biggest defence was Nea's constant and gigantic smile. It should be obvious that she wasn't frightened, I hoped.

The waitress returned with our drinks and turned to Nea.

'Kaikki hyvin?' she asked.

'Joo, kittos,' Nea answered.

The waitress said something else, pointing to a WC sign. Nea nodded and turned to her drink. The waitress hesitated, shot a glance at me, and returned behind the counter. If you need to use the bathroom it is right here, she must have said, meaning: if you need to get away from your kidnapper go in there and I'll follow and help you.

I sat, face burning, and tried to talk slowly and simply with Nea, asking her about school, her friends, the games she was playing. The waitress returned with our burgers, asked me this time if everything was all right, and disappeared again. The workers were now busy with more customers and were no longer staring. I relaxed, and Nea and I began eating. Nea worked with determination on a hamburger the size of a dachshund and I couldn't help but laugh. It looked like the Finnish Maiden had stepped out of a nineteenth-century painting to have lunch. She was the personification of the country, blond and pretty and dripping sisu.

'You're adorable, Nea,' I told her. 'I have fun spending time with you.'

'I love you!' she blurted out, a giant smile on her face.

I came around the table to give her a hug. As I sat down again Nea watched me expectantly. I looked down at my plate and took a bite of food. When I raised my eyes she was still looking at me. I smiled at her and tapped her fork playfully with my own. She stopped waiting and took another bite of her burger.

24

I took a photo of Nea gloriously gnawing on her giant burger and shared it on social media. The photo immediately received a comment from an acquaintance.

'How cute!' she wrote. 'Who is the little girl?'

Great question, I thought. What is my relationship with Nea? Technically she was my friends' child, but that explanation was inadequate. You don't spend an afternoon shopping with your friends' kid. I didn't think of Nea—or Minttu, or Niilo—solely as my friends' kids anyway. I was developing relationships with them as individuals, separate from my ties to Kaarle and Mari.

'That's my niece,' I replied.

A niece was probably the closest definition I could use to describe how I felt about Nea, but it wasn't a true statement. After the divorce Kaarle was no longer my brother-in-law, and it galled me to describe Nea in terms of my former wife. I was also worried what Nea's real family might say about my claim. They knew Nea wasn't my niece. They might wonder why I was spending the afternoon with her at all.

As Nea finished her burger and fries—and some of my fries—and got to work on her sundae I watched my phone to see if anyone would take umbrage at me being with her. Soon enough, Nea's grandmother and aunts gave thumbs-ups to the picture. They must have accepted me calling her a niece, at least for now. I breathed a tentative sigh of relief.

Nea had finished her sundae and was beginning to fidget.

'I'm stupid,' I told her. 'I'm wasting time on my phone and it's not like I get to see you every day. I promise: no more phones. You have my complete attention.'

Back to shopping. Nea deigned to look at nail polish, jewellery and toys, but she was mainly focused on clothes. Her shopping style wasn't impulsive. It was as careful and contemplative as a high court judge weighing the arguments of a landmark case. She tried on different items, comparing, contrasting, considering. Her face was a caricature of thinking. Nea's brow furrowed and she stared at nothing in the distance, holding a shirt in her hand. Decision made, her face relaxed and she checked her tiny change purse. A twenty-euro bill was neatly folded up in it, keeping company with a few coins.

'I'll buy it, sweetie,' I told her. 'Save your money for something else.'

Nea was happy to discover she wouldn't have to pay for her clothes and gave me another hug, but she didn't take advantage of someone with a fat wallet doting upon her. She judiciously picked out a pair of cheap shoes in another store but rejected my offer to buy a jacket and another shirt she was interested in.

I didn't know if Kaarle's warning about not letting her out of my sight was serious or not, but I took it seriously. The coffee at Kaarle and Mari's, coupled with the big Coke I had at the restaurant, had gathered uncomfortably in my bladder, but I didn't want to separate from Nea to go to the bathroom. I kept getting a nightmare image of a tall faceless man snatching her when I wasn't there. The image was vivid and disturbing, and I saw her being dragged away as she looked over her shoulder at me in horror. But finally I couldn't stand it any longer and we went to the bathrooms. I waited until she disappeared into the women's room and ran into the men's and peed as fast as I could. My handwashing was criminally perfunctory, and I stood outside the women's restroom wringing my hands with a low-grade terror that she had already come out and been snatched, until Nea emerged with a giant smile on her face. I was so relieved to see her I gave her another hug. She was safe. No faceless man was going to grab her on my watch.

'I have fun with you!' Nea said in a tone as if she had rehearsed her line.

'I have fun with you, too, but I wonder where your parents are.'

We had been shopping for hours and the afternoon was fading. I called Kaarle and learned he wasn't far away, looking for us in the mall. We rendezvoused at the bookstore.

'Everything go okay?' he asked.

'Everything went great,' I told him. 'Thanks for letting me spend the afternoon with her. We had a lot of fun.'

'No problem. Glad you enjoyed it.'

His smiling face became puzzled when I handed Nea her three shopping bags.

'Kuinka paljon rahaa käytit?' he asked her.

Nea gave a hurried explanation, displaying her bags as evidence and pointing at me.

Kaarle turned to me. He took a deep breath and opened his

mouth wide. But in the instant before he spoke Mari casually and calmly said a few words. Kaarle paused, slowly lowered the finger he had been about to jab into my chest and looked at her. She said something more, expanding or explaining on her statement as she smiled up at him.

I had no idea what Mari had said, but I could decipher the incident. Kaarle was angry that I had bought things for Nea, but before he could say anything Mari had waved it off as inconsequential. Kaarle and Mari were always united and never contradicted each other in front of their kids. I was lucky Mari happened to be the first one to speak. If it had been the other way around she wouldn't have defended me.

25

Saga was fluent in Swedish, but she wasn't much help in my education. She was a teacher and didn't want to do it in the evenings. Once her dog leapt up at me and I scolded it.

'Hoppar inte!' I told the dog.

Saga stared at me like she couldn't believe someone with my level of idiocy existed.

'It's *hoppa* inte,' she said disdainfully. 'Use the imperative.'

My Swedish skills were improving, but at a continental drift pace. My reading and writing were good enough that I could have simple email conversations about interviews, edits or articles, although I continued to rely heavily on dictionaries and Google Translate. I participated in online discussions and could find my way through to the gist of a *Hufvudstadsbladet* newspaper article. Yet my conversation skills were no better than when I had clumsily gone out to talk to people and met Saga. I needed to have conversations in Swedish with someone who would be willing to help me along, a private tutor.

I thought of Tapio, the man who had published two of my books. He was a respected editor and publisher in the Finnish-Swedish world and knew everyone in the community. He also had a daughter who was often on my island of Drumsö because her boyfriend lived there. She might be interested in helping me practice Swedish for an hour or so a week for some beer money.

'Hej Tapio,' I emailed him. 'How are things going? I have a request for you. I would like to find someone to practice Swedish with—such as for an hour a week over coffee. I'd be happy to pay for their time, as if they were an informal tutor. If you think of someone like this who might be interested in a bit of extra cash, would you keep me in mind? Hälsningar, David.'

'Hej David,' he replied. 'I'd like to do that myself. If it was an afternoon time it could work. I was educated to become a teacher a long time ago and even practiced as one. But would you like that? Glada hälsningar, Tapio.'

Yes, I would like that. Tapio wasn't merely a fluent speaker of the language, he worked and lived it. He had edited Swedish-language books that would go on to win the Finlandia Prize. I was surprised that someone so busy could find the time for something like this, but he liked me and he liked to teach so was happy to do it.

'Tja!' I tried to say at our first meeting at a café in Kampen. He gave me an uncertain smile.

'Tjanäre?' I tried again.

'Yes, you could use that,' he said, finally realising what I was trying to say, 'but that is more Riksvenska, meaning you are more likely to hear it in Sweden instead of in Finland. Hej is always a good greeting, and of course it sounds the same as Hei in Finnish.'

We bought some coffees and sat at a table where he briefly quizzed me to see my level of knowledge. I knew the words for cup, table and chair, but had no idea what to call a tray, wall or floor. Seeing that we needed to start at the beginning, we started at the beginning.

Tapio gave me a quick lesson on greetings, what to say for hellos (hej, godmorgon), goodbyes (hej då, adjö), polite small talk (Är du frisk?—Jag är frisk.) and if you wanted to give hints to continue the conversation (Hur mår du?—Inte så bra, tyvärr.). Much of my online self-study had been with materials from Sweden and I soon learned that Finnish Swedish was different.

‘Don’t worry about that sing-song prosody,’ he told me. ‘They speak like that in Riksvenska, but not so much here in Finland. Finns speak more in a monotone so it will be easier for you. You’ll always have an accent so just work on getting the words right.

‘We have our own phrases, too. If someone says “Hur går det?” to you here in Finland you can always answer “Som surt brinner”. That is a very Finnish-Swedish phrase and people will smile to hear you say it.’

‘Som surt brinner,’ I practiced, writing it down. ’What does it mean?’

‘A literal translation would be as something wet burns, but it means “so-so”, in a slightly humorous or self-deprecating way,’ said Tapio. ‘It would be like in America if someone asked “How are things going?” and you answered “Hangin’ in there.”’

We met every week, but I was busy and frequently tried to cancel. Tapio was tenacious and refused to let me skip lessons. If I wanted to speak the language I had to speak the language. It needed to be a priority, and if that meant rescheduling appointments or delaying article submissions then that is what I needed to do. Tapio’s job is to hold a writer’s feet in the fire until she talked (or wrote, to be precise), and he did the same thing to me. Tapio was as busy as I was, and had a more demanding job, but was willing to juggle his schedule to fit mine. He was serious about teaching me Swedish and this made me serious about learning it.

During our weekly meetings at the café in Kampen we spoke about what we had been doing and events in the news. We only used Swedish, even including ordering coffees from the flustered waitresses, unless we needed to clarify something. I had the ubiquitous student problem of thinking in English and translating it into Swedish, which he worked to correct.

‘You say “I go fishing” in English, but you don’t say “Jag går fiske" in Swedish,' he told me. 'People would understand what you mean, but it sounds strange. Think of gå like walking. Jag går till affären. I go, or walk, to the store. You don't gå to Sicily for holiday. You reser to Sicily, travel to Sicily. You don't gå fishing. Instead say "Jag fiskar". I fish.'

I also learned how closely English and Swedish were related, particular in the modern spoken language.

'Jag skriver en artikel om...om...what is "big data" in Swedish?' I asked one day.

'Big data.'

'Yes, what is it in Swedish? Stora. . .besked?'

'No, it is the same. We say "big data" in Swedish. Many newer phrases like that are borrowed directly from English.'

'Oh, okay,' I said, and continued. 'Jag skriver en artikel om big data men jag har ett...ett...what is "problem"?'

'Problem.'

'The same word again?'

'Yes, they're the same. If you don't know the word in Swedish, say it in English. Everyone knows English so they will understand what you mean. Also, if you are lucky the word is the same in both languages. Swedish has many English loanwords and the two languages share many cognates. You just need to pronounce it the Swedish way.'

My pronunciation was catastrophically bad, my sentences were characterised by long pauses as I searched for words, and I had to constantly ask people to repeat themselves, but over time I could actually communicate in spoken Swedish. It wasn't pretty, but it was working.

Once I overheard a telephone conversation from a girl planning to meet her friend at a restaurant, and I was in awe that I understood exactly what she was saying. Another time I was in the kitchen and stopped kneading my bread so I could clearly hear the weather forecast on YLE radio Vega, and the fact that I could comprehend what the woman was saying (cloudy tomorrow, cloudy the next day) struck me harder than the forecast.

Yet the more I learned the more I understood how much I needed to learn. I had always given a condescending smile to Finns who couldn't get English prepositions correct, but after delving into Swedish prepositions I no longer smiled. Till, för, med, på, vid, hos, av, i…they chaotically swirled around my mind banging everything off my mental shelves. I took tests in workbooks where sometimes ninety per cent of the prepositions I used were wrong. How the fuck do I walk 'till' the store but I walk 'på' the theatre? If there were some logical system to it all I couldn't find it.

The homework which Tapio gave me every week varied greatly. Near May Day he had me speak with his mother over the phone about how to make mjöd, or mead, the traditional drink for that time of year. To learn past tense I had to write stories about historical events ('För…sedan,' he stressed. 'People always make that mistake.'). To learn future tense I had to make predictions about the future ('No, no, no. You use ska here and kommer att here. Think of ska like an intention or plan for the future, but kommer att like a natural process or logical progression. You can also use present tense and qualify your meaning. Jag äter pizza i morgon. I am eating pizza tomorrow.).'

The weeks passed and I told him about my various adventures in trying to use Swedish in my everyday life. Sometimes I needed to use Swedish in my work, like when I accidently stumbled into translating an entire Swedish website into English for one of my clients.

'Bra!' Tapio nodded approvingly.

'Men jag pratar inte svenska!' I told him, worried that I wasn't up to the task.

'Du pratar svenska,' he told me sternly. 'Let's see if you can really translate something into English.'

The next week he gave me the 'Shame' chapter from Rafael Donner's book, *Människan är ett känsligt djur*. This wasn't just a regular homework assignment, but a test. I approached it seriously, as if it was a freelance job, and worked on it for hours. In one sentence Donner had used a sophisticated rhythm and rhyming scheme. Maintaining the rhyme, rhythm and meaning simultaneously was impossible, so I tried to find a careful balance. I decided what the author said took priority, but I would make a few sacrifices to demonstrate how he had said it.

Man slår sig, faller, fäller, har sönder, sliter, tappar, glömmer, missar stöter, snubblar, sjabblar och famlar.

You get hit, fall, get knocked down, break, wear out, lose, forget, miss, get bruised, stumble, fumble and tumble.

When I apprehensively turned in the three-thousand-word translation Tapio only edited a single word. He said that the publishing house might even use it to show Donner's book to international publishers. I was astonished.

'Jag behövde en ordbok,' I confessed to my crime.

'Det är okej,' Tapio said, but suddenly had a thought and looked doubtful. 'Varje ord?'

'Nej, men varje mening.'

He waved it off as inconsequential that I had needed a dictionary and told me my homework for next week was to write a poem in Swedish. I am no poet, so tried to disguise my lack of skills with humour.

Min svenska handledare är grov
Han gav mig ett svårt prov
Skriv en dikt som han sa,
Och den borde vara bra
En rimordbok är nu ett behov.

'Bra!' Tapio laughed and gave me ten points out of ten for being funny despite my mistakes, which is how life works.

Our time for that week was up, and I needed to hurry home to finish writing another article. We gathered up our things, called 'tack' to the baristas who were used to us by now and walked down the corridor to the Ben & Jerry's ice cream kiosk. I turned to go to the metro and Tapio headed for the exit.

'Tack så mycket,' I called over the widening gap between us. 'Det var roligt.'

'Tack själv. Jag tyckte om det också,' he said. 'Nästa torsdag?'

'Ja. Vi ses!'

'Vi ses!'

Hurrying commuters glanced at us curiously as we yelled to each other across the Kampen caverns. They are not staring at me for being a foreigner speaking English, I thought. For the first time, Finns are staring at me for speaking Swedish. I wondered if it was an improvement. Well, it is a change, at least, and that is what I am looking for.

26

One day late that summer Kaarle invited me to take a ride on his new boat, the *Minttu III.* Every few years he and Mari upgraded boats and now had a larger cabin cruiser.

'Fuel is really expensive, so I thought we could just take a short trip,' he said.

I stood on the dock and chatted with Minttu and Nea as Kaarle worked to unsnap and roll up the soft top covering the boat's deck. An elderly couple were on the sailboat next to his. Their sailboat had a few yachting club flags fluttering in the wind, as well as the red and gold pendant of the Swedish-speaking Finns. The lady was struggling to climb down from the deck to the dock with her hands filled with bags.

'Kan jag hjälpa dig? Jag kan ta påsarna,' I said, and held out my hands for her bags.

Both Kaarle's and the lady's eyes widened in surprise that I had spoken Swedish, and I was rather surprised myself. I'm really doing it, I thought. For the first time I can actually communicate with Finns in their own language.

Still beaming, I sat on the padded bench on the side of the deck between Minttu and Nea as Kaarle piloted us out a long, scenic waterway from his harbour. When we passed another boat everyone waved, acknowledging that we were in the same society of boaters. I felt a sense of belonging I hadn't felt in so long that I had forgotten what it was like. I stretched out my arms over the girls' shoulders. Minttu wasn't fond of public displays of affection and stayed stiffly erect but Nea snuggled close.

The clear blue sky was polka-dotted with a few soft white clouds. On the green islands and hills above the channel were everything from rustic red summer cabins to giant, modern holiday homes.

How egalitarian, I thought. Just like Finland itself.

'Harry Harkimo owns that one,' Kaarle yelled over the wind, pointing to a huge building with massive glass walls overlooking the water. 'He's the guy who owns the Jokerit hockey team.'

The girls were content to watch the scenery for only fifteen minutes before they asked if I wanted to go play cards in the cabin. I said yes and abandoned Kaarle to stand on the deck alone. I won one hand, Nea won two, and Minttu won the rest. Nea got upset and threw the cards at her sister, but a hug and a tickle from me got a smile back on her face. This was so wonderful: getting out on the water and spending time with the girls. I couldn't stop smiling.

Kaarle called me out to the deck when we entered our destination harbour to help him tie up. As soon as I climbed the steep steps back to the deck and saw him alone at the wheel I cringed at myself. This was my friend, who had invited me to spend time on his boat with him, but I had rejected him for his daughters. He had reached out to me after the divorce when I really needed him, but now I ignore him for someone better.

But he brought his girls along, I told myself, and he knows how much we like each other. Maybe he doesn't mind, and is even encouraging us to develop relationships. This was a flimsy justification to ignore him and focus upon his daughters, but it helped to ease my conscience.

I inexpertly helped Kaarle tie the boat up at the dock and we walked to the harbour café. This was how they spent their summers, leisurely cruising from one guest harbour to the next along the coast. It was a wonderful Finnish custom—taking a month or so off to enjoy the natural beauty of the country—but one in which I didn't participate. I only worked.

We picked out ice creams and I also grabbed a beer. Standing in the queue for the cash register Kaarle suddenly shifted from foot to foot, slapped his pockets and looked around plaintively like he was searching for some way to escape. In a rare bit of insight I realised that he had forgotten his money.

'I'll buy it,' I said, moving in front of him and the girls. 'Thanks for taking me out today.'

The cashier rang up the four ice creams and beer and I plucked a bill out of my wallet. Minttu, who stayed so close to me that she might have been mistaken as my conjoined twin, let out a surprised laugh.

'You're paying with a fifty!' she said.

'Well, the only bills I have are fifties.'

We sat at a picnic table in the sun to eat our ice creams. Kaarle explained a bit about the Finnish boating life and I told him what I had been doing recently.

'I have to give a talk to some business students from North Carolina at Aalto University Monday. They are here to study Finnish companies and they asked me to talk about Nokia,' I said. 'Then I have two different CEOs to interview later during the week. Oh, yeah. I also have a meeting with the BBC who are here for a story on Finland.'

'Goddamn you have your shit together,' Kaarle said. 'You're doing something right.'

Up until the second he said that I would have thought the same thing. But was this it? I looked at my life and didn't find anything. It was so empty, so meaningless compared to his life. Yes, my wallet was full of fifties but his home was full of family members. There was some deep unease in me, something which had been there a long time, which I just now recognised.

27

Life was on autopilot. I got up at six am every day and was working by seven. I called editors and interviewees, wrote articles, edited them, got feedback, submitted them and made invoices. I meditated and exercised and practiced Swedish. Sometimes I travelled for meetings, going downtown or out to Otnäs to talk with communications staffers or interview people with 'Chief' in their titles. Receptionists looked doubtfully at my shaggy, shoulder-length hair but executives were almost always welcoming and even delighted with how I looked. I was a professional writer and was supposed to be eccentric. If I couldn't write there was no way I would dare to show up looking like that. I am a writer, I lied. Look at me.

Every day I abandoned my phone on my desk and went outside to walk for an hour. Sometimes it was in the morning; sometimes it was in the evening. It depended upon my schedule but I always did it, no matter the weather. I bought a raincoat and spiked boots so I could walk in the grey rain or on the grey ice which blanketed Finland for most of the year.

I walked and I thought. I thought about old friends, old loves, old dogs. I thought about everything I had accomplished. I was making more money than I could spend. I had a girlfriend, of sorts, or at least an intimate relationship with a woman. I could see some progress with my Swedish skills, unlike in my years of effort with Finnish. I had friendships with Robert and Kaarle, and even entirely different relationships: my siblings had never had kids, but with Kaarle's children I had people who I considered nieces and nephews. My exercising had put me in better shape than I had been in fifteen years or more. I meditated regularly, read great literature, ate healthily, explored nature, limited brain-melting online time, kept a meticulous home and avoided accumulating material crap. Everything was perfect and I was becoming more and more unhappy.

I didn't want any of this. I had thought that if I could

accomplish all these things then I would be fulfilled, but I had been wrong. I felt like I was doing the wrong things, as if I was hurrying to some destination only to slowly realise that I might have been going the wrong direction.

'Might have been' were the operative words, because I wasn't sure. I couldn't get Kaarle's statement out of my mind. 'Goddamn you have your shit together,' he had said. 'You're doing something right.'

By the standards of modern society I suppose I was doing something right. If I were to sit down with a psychiatrist or psychologist I wouldn't know what to say. I had none of the conventional problems of people in modern society.

Well, except one. I was alone. I couldn't let my relationships with Saga or Robert or Nea fool me into thinking I was anything but alone. When the next March rolled around I once again flew to Sicily so I would have an excuse why I was spending my birthday alone. Yet being alone was exactly what I had wanted. During the last years of my marriage the happiest moments I had were when Heljä left to visit her mother for a few days. I had always lied and said I had too much work to do and couldn't go, and as soon as she left and closed the door a giant smile broke across my face. Yes, I had thought in glee, finally I'm alone. I needed to be alone for something, but I didn't know what.

28

Nea's birthday was 28 February. Minttu was born on 24 March, one day before me. The close proximity of their birthdays meant that Kaarle and Mari threw a joint party for both of them, which this year was delayed until early summer because they had been so busy during the spring. Kaarle sent out a mass SMS to friends and family, inviting them to come, but my invitation came from Nea, who had seized responsibility for keeping me up to date with her family's events.

'Will Heljä be there?' I messaged Kaarle.

'She won't be here,' he said.

'Then I'll come.'

I was excited. The girls were always happy at parties, with the food and crowds and bustle, and I liked to see them happy. Neither Minttu nor Nea could think of anything in particular they wanted, so I checked with Kaarle. Just a card and some money would be fine, he said. I went to the grocery store and picked out two Swedish-language birthday cards. When I got home I looked in my wallet and considered how much to give them. They wanted for nothing, but Kaarle and Mari were strict about money. Minttu had told me that they received no allowance, but would only be given money for specific purposes. I liked the girls very much and wanted to give them something that would surprise them and allow them to splurge a bit. I picked out two new, crisp bills from my wallet and sealed them inside the birthday cards.

It was one of the warmest days of the year and everyone was outside on Kaarle and Mari's terrace. I had been worried about the cop-out of only giving money instead of taking the time to buy gifts, but practically everyone had brought cards. The girls sat down on the wooden deck and began opening their loot. Most of the child guests were on the trampoline or running through the green grass. The majority of the adults were on the terrace, although Mari and her mother were inside preparing food in the kitchen.

Nea opened a card, read it, and took out a grey five-euro bill.

'Thanks, Grandpa!' she said in Finnish, and Grandpa got a hug. Minttu followed suit, getting a card and a five and giving a hug.

The girls each opened another card and stacked their respective five-euro bills.

'Thanks, Aunt Heidi!' they said one after another. Aunt Heidi got hugs.

Another card, another five.

'Thanks, Grandma!'

I squirmed in my chair, trying to get comfortable. Suddenly I was assailed by doubts. Five euros seemed to be the common opinion of what was appropriate to give little girls for their birthdays, but I had smashed through that barrier with a sledgehammer. Finns frown upon people being different, people breaking the accepted rules of society, people bragging and drawing attention to themselves American-fashion, but that is exactly what I was doing.

Nea opened my card and the orange fifty-euro bill fluttered out to lie on her crossed legs. She ignored it to read the card, carefully put the bill aside, and came to give me a hug. She tried and failed to supress her giant smile in order to show only a suitable amount of pleasure. Minttu was next. She read the Swedish text and below where I had written in English: 'Happy Birthday kulta! David.' Over her head I saw the adults' eyes looking at the bill on the wooden deck.

The adults avoided looking at me. Everyone was stiff, except for the laughing kids on the lawn.

When the last card was opened, the last five stacked with the others, and the last hug given, Kaarle casually walked to stand over Nea. I heard a quiet question and a quiet answer, but the only thing I understood was Nea saying my name. Kaarle walked over to me.

'What are you doing?' he asked.

'Oh, it's nothing. Let me spoil them. Isn't that an uncle's job?'

'You aren't their uncle.'

He turned and walked away as the adults pretended to look elsewhere. I sat, face burning, trying and failing to appear unconcerned and wishing Mari had been there to defend me. The girls knew very well what had happened. Minttu refused to look at me. She was Daddy's girl and craved his approval. If Kaarle was displeased Minttu was displeased. Their opinions were one and the same. Nea was more of a rebel. She shot me a look of sympathy, hurried to her room to stash her cards and cash, and ran back out straight to me. Nea grabbed my hand, pulled me out of my chair and dragged me into the yard to play.

I had fun playing with the kids, as always, but the episode with the money ate at me. I wanted to leave and go home, but the idea of skulking away was as painful as enduring the careful silence from all the adults. I stayed until after the cake and coffee and then said I needed to go write. That is the perfect excuse to get out of everything. People only have a vague idea of what writers do, so they give us a great deal of leeway. Normally at these gatherings I was the last to leave; now I would be one of the first.

When I tried to tell Nea goodbye she ushered me into her room and closed the door so we were alone. She went to her desk and picked up her birthday cards which she had hidden under a pile of notebooks. Nea pulled out the fifty-euro-bill I had given her and displayed it to me.

'It's okay,' she assured me. 'It's okay.'

Her English was dreadful, but she managed to communicate the essentials. I gave her a hug and kissed the top of her head and went to say goodbye to Minttu in her room. As Minttu and I were following the necessary steps of the traditional goodbye conversation Kaarle casually appeared. He glanced around and spotted Minttu's pile of cash on her dresser. With a smile on his face, he teasingly snatched the fifty from her pile and stuck it in his pocket. Minttu leapt up with a cry of pretended outrage and Kaarle laughingly gave it back.

'You should hide that so no one steals it,' I told Minttu.

'Yeah, you should!' Kaarle said.

His voice was strained, like he was trying too hard to be cheerful. He was still bothered by the incident but was trying to downplay it. This was hard for him as well. I had embarrassed Kaarle and Mari's family by showing them up in the gifts department, and maybe I had embarrassed Kaarle and Mari as well. In effect I had said: your family only gave you a pittance, but look at what I can do. Look how much better I am. Look at me!

Minttu was of that age that she was embarrassed to show

affection in front of others, but this time she took it to extremes. With her father present she only reluctantly gave me a goodbye hug, ostentatiously turning her face as far away from me as possible, as if the very act of touching me was distasteful. I had upset her Daddy and so I had upset her, and she made sure I knew it. Enduring the contempt from Minttu was the most painful thing in the entire episode. She had always been my special buddy but was now making it clear where the limits of our relationship were drawn.

Fine, I thought. I didn't see you offer to return the fifty, you hypocrite. Take your fucking hugs elsewhere. See if I care. I still have Nea.

Normally when I left Minttu saw me to the door, but this time Kaarle did. He fidgeted out in the driveway as if there were more things to say but he didn't know how to do it, so I did it for him.

'I don't have a family, you know. Well, I do, but they are thousands of miles away,' I said. 'Money is the only thing I can offer your kids. I have nothing they need. I need them, but they don't need me.'

Kaarle sighed and looked off into the trees for a moment before again making eye contact with me.

'You're wrong,' he said. 'Just don't spoil them.'

29

After the divorce I had moved to a unique place. The island of Drumsö was almost exactly in the centre of the greater Helsingfors area, but it was like a little village. There were charming houses with miniature apple orchards, old wooden sailboats bobbing in harbours, neighbours chatting over fences and great swaths of land designated as forest. No wonder the rents were so high. It was a fantastic place to live, but the seasons were turning.

Helsingfors' long-delayed metro expansion would put two new stations on the northern edge of the island. In keeping with the development plan, all areas around the stations would be built up as thickly as possible. This meant cutting every plot of trees that they could and then changing green space protection rules so they could cut down more. The city contractors were brutally efficient. People went downtown to work in the morning and returned to find their favourite picnic spot had been clearcut for a new apartment complex. Not only were the trees down, they were gone, already trucked away to the lumber and pulp mills. The only reminder of what had once been were stumps and the deep tyre tracks in the mud from the forestry equipment.

Trees weren't the only things that were being cut. When the long-delayed metro finally opened the public transit authority took a chainsaw to the bus services. To make up for the cuts the city graciously allowed us to pay extra to ride their city bikes to the metro stations. Fuck that, I thought, and walked through the rain and mud and slush.

The cut in public transportation was inevitable. Helsingfors was struggling in the era of austerity and they had wasted an enormous sum of money during the botched metro construction. I will probably never see public services expanded in my lifetime, so it was time to take care of myself. For the first time since I moved to Finland I seriously considered buying a car.

'Why do you need a car?' Saga asked. 'You work from home. You live only a few blocks from the stores. You walk to my place.'

'I might write from home, but several times a week I need to travel for appointments.'

'To where?'

'Mostly in the city. Downtown or Esbo.'

'Espoo,' she corrected me, rolling her eyes. She wasn't fond of my habit of using Swedish place names. 'So you'll buy a car to drive ten kilometres a few times a week?'

Saga had a point. Yet there was another alternative. A number of companies saw Helsingfors' cuts in public transportation and realised they had an opportunity. Almost overnight cars began to appear on Drumsö streets with modest signs on them with words of mobility and immediacy, such as Go, Drive and Now. Carsharing services had arrived.

This would be perfect, I thought. I'd have the convenience of a car without any of the hassle of ownership. I signed up for the most popular carsharing service and was delighted with how much time I saved. I used to budget an hour to travel to an appointment in Vantaa, but now could do it in twenty minutes.

Having access to a car also made it easier to visit Robert and Kaarle. I frequently drove to the west to see Robert, where we fished or wandered the forest. Robert was a great campfire cook, and I spent hours with him learning how to find, prepare and preserve the bounty of the Finnish land and lakes. To the east was Kaarle, or, more precisely, Kaarle's kids.

I no longer made up excuses to see the kids, but openly asked if I could do something with them. It began by taking Minttu and Nea to see the Nutcracker ballet and soon I was doing something with one of them about once a month. In the beginning every meeting was thoroughly dissected and considered—where are you going, what are you doing, message us when you get there, when will you be home—but over time I was given more freedom. Every request, whether it came from me or one of the kids, was approved with no conditions.

Slowly our relationship was redefined so that my primary contacts were the kids, and Kaarle and Mari became secondary. During a typical visit I spent five minutes chatting with Kaarle and five hours with the kids. Sometimes I didn't even see Kaarle and Mari. They would be out running errands, having left Elias or Mari's parents in charge. Once Nea and I were going to a water park and when I arrived she charged down the hill and leaped into the passenger seat, ready to immediately leave.

'If I'm taking a father's little girl out for the day the least I should do is talk to him before we leave,' I told her.

'Mitä?' Nea asked, already buckled in.

Nea preferred physical activities like swimming pools and activity parks. Niilo was more selective. He turned down many things which I thought he would enjoy, like fishing or going to see rally races, but he did like laser tag and arcades. Minttu was easiest. She would do anything I suggested and often had her own ideas for our activities.

Once I asked Niilo if he wanted to see a hockey game. He said no, but Minttu had heard our conversation and said that she would like to go. I took her to a Jokerit game on a Saturday and we returned just as the family were going to their nightly sauna. They asked me to come with them, and Minttu gushed about the experience in the warm, dim room.

'David bought Club Seats, in the fifth row!' Minttu said. 'And we got mozzarella sticks!'

Mari smiled and congratulated her on our wonderful night, but Kaarle was silent and his smile was a grimace in the flickering light from the sauna stove.

The girls loved shopping, yet they had been warned that there was a limit on what they could accept from me. They allowed me to buy a few things but quickly started refusing my offers to buy more. Yet one summer Minttu asked for and received special dispensation for me to splurge on her back-to-school purchases. She was mature and dependable, often called upon by her parents to perform special chores at home, and so was rewarded privileges on rare occasions. I don't know what favours she called in from her parents, but after negotiations were successfully concluded she sent me a message surrounded by smiling emojis: 'This time I will let you buy me things.'

We went to Stockmann's and bought makeup, clothes, accessories and sports outfits for her gym classes. I spent so much money that I began confiscating the sales receipts and warned her not to keep track.

'Why did Daddy tell you not to spoil me?' Minttu asked.

'I don't know,' I half-lied.

I tried to find things to do the kids would enjoy, but sometimes I tried to push them into activities that I wanted them to like. Kaarle and Mari were not readers, and so none of the kids were either, but on a whim I gave Minttu a Finnish-language version of *The Hobbit*. The book had been given to me by a special aunt when I was her age and over time had become my all-time favourite. I'm eternally grateful for that aunt who gave it to me and I wanted to recreate that experience with Minttu.

The book is a dated for today's society, with its all-male cast and 19th-Century social stratification, but it is still one of the world's great stories. I wasn't sure she could work through it, being so addicted to media displayed through a phone screen as she was. She gave me regular updates as she read it over several weeks before references to the book in her messages dried up. She claimed she had finished it, but I prudently didn't ask her any questions about the narrative.

Nea couldn't speak much English, but we could communicate through signs and simple sentences. Sometimes a pain went through me as Nea got frustrated and embarrassed as she struggled to tell me something. What good is your Swedish now, I wondered. Sure, you can ask a waitress in Mariehamn where the bathroom is, but you can't talk to this little girl. You want to talk with her like you do with her brother and sister, but you can't. Every time I looked at Nea I smiled—I continued to think of her as the Finnish Maiden—but the smile was always bittersweet. I knew our relationship had a natural limit to how far it could evolve, simply because we couldn't communicate properly.

It was different with Niilo and Minttu. Niilo was impressively fluent with English and we had long conversations about everything from games to his friends at school. Minttu was almost like a different person when she was alone with me. She was normally reserved, but the instant we were alone she began to pour out her thoughts and feelings as if they had been tied up inside and now finally could be set free.

Minttu told me things ranging from the mundane to the serious, like funny incidents at school or her feelings about her biological father. She told me about a friend who was born a girl but felt more like a boy. ('FTM,' I murmured sagely as Minttu glanced at me in confusion.) Sometimes she veered into deeply personal topics, such as when she astonished me by talking about her rapidly developing body. I didn't know what to say to a teenage girl about periods, growing boobs and expanding hips, but luckily she didn't expect me to say anything. One of the greatest lessons Finland taught me is how silence is the most important part of a conversation. I was silent, listened and tried to understand her.

She's opening up because she trusts me, I thought. She truly likes me and we really are friends.

'You can talk to me about anything,' I told her one day as she sat in the passenger seat of my rented car. 'As far as I'm concerned nothing is off limits.'

'Thank you,' Minttu said. 'But I already know that.'

Our ritual of long private conversations was inviolate. Every time I was at their house Minttu invited me back to her room and closed the door so we could talk. These conversations even happened during big parties with thirty people present. She shooed five or six cousins and siblings out of her room so she and I could talk alone. All the adults smiled to see her clear out a private space for us and none of the kids complained. Everyone knew we were close and everyone respected our privacy.

Except Kaarle. He would always interrupt at some point, just to check on us. After ten seconds of 'Everything good in here?' he would leave again and even close the door behind him. Maybe it was the natural fatherly instinct to check on his teenage daughter when she was alone in a bedroom with a man. Maybe it was something else, too.

After one particularly long conversation Minttu and I left her room to find Kaarle in the hallway, as if he had been waiting. Minttu walked past him to go outside to the rest of the family, but

I stopped and studied his face. It was like porcelain under stress, ready to shatter.

'I'm so happy that she talks to you,' Kaarle said in a tight voice. 'I'm very happy that she has you as a friend and an adult that she will talk to.'

But doesn't she talk to you? I wanted to ask, but didn't dare. I didn't want to put any strain on that porcelain face.

30

There was a lot of demand for writers like me. Finnish and Swedish companies need to look abroad because their domestic markets are so small, and the international language of business is English. However, there aren't many native English writers who specialise in telling the world about what we are doing up here in the land of clouds and frozen mud. In a relatively short amount of time I amassed an impressive list of bluechip clients and my collection of non-disclosure agreements symbolised a hefty chunk of the OMX Nordic stock market capitalisation.

These big corporations, as well as major public institutions, came to trust me after a time of working together. I would receive a call: 'Interview our CEO about this,' they would say, and leave everything else up to me. I came to understand each group's individual culture and adapted my writing to the organisation. Swedish companies were more American-style arrogant and flamboyant, and in fact preferred US English. Finnish groups wanted a more neutral, journalistic tone and tended to use the UK English style. I could flip my writing between in-your-face Swedish boasting to humble Finnish reporting simply by opening a new Word document and kicking my mental process into the correct gear.

I rarely had ethical considerations regarding my role as a mercenary writer—or 'literary hooker' as Robert termed it—but that was only because my personal beliefs and professional tasks tended to match. I honestly believe that Nordic companies make fantastic elevators, ship engines and software, for example, so I was more than happy to write articles saying so. I'm convinced that Finland's education system is fantastic and tourists should come see the country's forests and archipelagos, so I eagerly sang their praises to an international audience. Occasionally, though, I was asked to write stories that were problematic.

One editor asked me to find some random hip, urban young woman and interview her about why she loved a venerable and famous Finnish fashion house. I didn't know the slightest thing about fashion so called up Kaarle's cousin Liisa, the hippest urban young woman I knew, and invited her for coffee.

Liisa is a black hole, irresistibly pulling in the attention of every person around her. She has the body of a Greek goddess, night black hair (when it isn't green or purple), gigantic tattoos screaming across her chest and huge dark eyes reminiscent of Japanese cartoon characters. Her dangerous makeup looks like it was applied with a switchblade. She effortlessly wore clothes that would make the rebel designers of New York or Milan salivate. If anyone knew about urban fashion it was her, and thirty seconds into our conversation I realised I had a problem.

'My teachers wear that brand!' Liisa said, the piercings in her face shaking in horror. 'I would never wear them!'

'Do any of your friends like them?'

'My mom does.'

My British acquaintance Dick might be able to help, I thought. His teenaged daughters were hip and fashionable, based upon their Instagram pictures. The older girl had even done some modelling for local designers. Dick's girls were more commercial and less avant-garde than Liisa so might be a better choice. I called him and asked if they ever wore that famous Finnish brand or had any friends who did.

'Hell if I know,' he said. 'But I'll go and ask.'

Phone in his hand, Dick walked through the house and knocked on his daughters' door. They invited him in and he asked if they had any clothes from that fashion house. A second of stunned silence was followed by howls of laughter.

'Emmi has ten shopping bags of them!' I heard a gleeful voice shout.

'Elli is wearing them right now!'

The mutual accusations and laughter were muffled as Dick backed out and closed their door.

'No, they don't wear any of their stuff,' he told me unnecessarily.

I called my editor.

'I'm going to be honest with you,' I said. 'I don't think we can do this interview. Hip, urban young women don't like this brand.'

'Of course they do!' she said indignantly.

'Great! Tell me one you know and I'll interview her.'

My suggestion was greeted by the silence of painful realisation.

'Just write that fashionable young women love the brand,' my editor snapped. 'You don't need to interview anyone.'

I was making more than enough money, but it was still hard to turn down a job. If I said no they would find another freelancer and never come back. I wouldn't only lose the few hundred euros from this article—I would lose the uncounted thousands in the future from jobs that this editor would never send me. I told myself that surely there were fashionable young women somewhere who liked the brand, so I wasn't lying (probably), and gritted my teeth to write the story.

Sometimes publications contacted me for completely unrealistic articles. An organisation called me when the author of *A Song of Ice and Fire,* George R.R. Martin, visited Finland. He came to Helsinki for the annual global fantasy and comic convention and generated a lot of excitement among the fantasy-loving Finns.

'A few years ago Martin visited Finland and wrote nice things about the country on his blog,' the editor explained. 'We want you to interview him about how much he loves Finland. It will be great promotion for the country. Maybe the title can be "Game of Thrones author George R.R. Martin loves Finland" or something like that. Those are great keywords for search engine optimisation.'

'I doubt I could get an interview,' I said. 'Not counting J.K. Rowling, Martin is probably the biggest author in the world right now. He could dictate stories to the BBC, New York Times or Xinhua. I can't imagine he will be interested in a little Finnish website. I promise to ask for an interview, but you must not expect one.'

I contacted someone who I judged to be the assistant of the assistant of Martin's publicist. He seemed rather amused that I would even ask.

'We get a lot of requests for interviews, you know,' he said kindly to my backwoods Finnish naiveté.

'I'm sure you do, but it can't hurt to ask. Who knows? Maybe you will say yes.'

'Well, we'll see.'

He sounded like a polite supermodel trying not to break the heart of the ugliest nerd who ever got the gumption to ask her out. I knew there was no way in hell Martin would talk to us so immediately forgot the article, which was a good thing because Martin's people immediately forgot it too.

Once I was contracted to write an article for a large Finnish food and confectionary company. They wanted a story about what they were doing to reduce food waste. This was important to them, not only to save money but also to put less stress on the environment.

This was an instance where my professional and personal opinions meshed perfectly. I was fanatical about not wasting food. One reason was because I had been low on money for so long and couldn't afford to waste food, but another reason was that there just seemed something morally wrong about discarding something people needed to survive.

Sometimes I went to absurd lengths to avoid throwing away

food. I had been on a romaine salad kick for a while and had bought a bag of red onions. After a number of meals I ate everything but the onions, which I forgot about. When I remembered them they were going soft and a few had already started to rot. I regretfully threw away the rotten ones and then cut up the remainder. I threw them into a big bowel, splashed them with olive oil, tossed in some croutons and had an entire meal of red onions. Saga cursed me for that for two days.

With my personal convictions firmly behind the corporate line I eagerly jumped into the food waste story. One interviewee was a mid-level Finnish executive in charge of their sustainability. She talked about their sustainability report a great deal, as well as some seminar she hosted for a handful of other mid-level managers in the company about not wasting food.

The other interviewee was the manager of one of their restaurants in Sweden. I interviewed him about the steps he took to first measure and then combat food wastage. It was fascinating. As he talked about weighing and recording food they had to discard I wondered what the average family would think if they did the same thing. The manager explained about proper ordering and menu management, how one type of food could be used in novel ways, how their guests were encouraged to take everything they wanted but eat everything they took. Moreover, he was a fantastic interviewee. He gave perfect quotes: useful and funny and unexpected and instructive. He was the type of interviewee writers dream about.

It was a fun article to write and I was happy with what I sent to the two interviewees for their approval before I could send it to the corporate communications department. The Swedish manager only had a few corrections and clarifications, but I received a call from the Finnish executive.

'I think there was a misunderstanding about what this article is supposed to be about,' she said. 'The main point is supposed to be the seminar we had. You led with the Swedish manager and had entirely too many quotes from him.'

'The Swedish restaurant is doing interesting and important things, concrete actions which directly affect your bottom line and your sustainability goals. This is a great story which everyone can relate to, and it paints your company in a fantastic light.'

'The article is about our sustainability seminar,' she said firmly. 'You need to lead with me, and the conclusion needs to be me. You can have a few quotes from him but only if they support the seminar.'

'Okay. So what actions did you take in the seminar?'

'We discussed reducing food waste. We talked about many interesting ideas which I've already told you about.'

'Yes, but what concrete actions came out of it? How did they benefit the company and the environment?'

She thought for a moment.

'Our snack during the seminar was day-old food from the cafeteria which would otherwise had been thrown away!' she said triumphantly.

I put my head in my hand.

'All right,' I said.

She sent me an email reiterating how the article was about their seminar, which wasn't accomplishing anything, and not about the Swedish restaurant, which was accomplishing something. She also made a point that the Swedish manager's quotes should be reduced and hers should be expanded.

I rewrote the article downplaying the good things the Swedish restaurant was doing and emphasising all the useless bureaucracy and meetings and discussions. To pay her back I employed a few writers' tricks, such as using strong active statements for the restaurant and passive weasel words for the seminar.

'The restaurant cut waste by thirty per cent...'

'Claims by the seminar participants include...'

To complete my petty revenge I sent this revised article to

both her and the Swedish manager, forwarded with the email she had written ordering that she should be the star of the story and the manager should be demoted to a supporting role. I wanted the manager to see exactly what she had said.

The mid-level executive hesitatingly approved this new version. The content was exactly what she wanted, but she couldn't quite figure out why it wasn't the trumpets-blazing panegyric for bureaucracy like she had hoped. She knew her seminar was being ridiculed but it was so subtle that she didn't understand how I was doing it. There was nothing she could point to and say 'change this' because I had written exactly what she had told me to write.

The Swedish restaurant manager never replied. He knew exactly what was happening. The company had a sustainability officer because they were required to have a sustainability officer. Her days were spent holding seminars for other mid-level executives who had nothing better to do and writing reports which were only read by the people paid to proofread them. He had been excited and happy to share the positive things his team was doing, but as soon as the corporate bullshit began to fly he stepped away and kept his head down. I don't blame him.

I was furious. This had been a fantastic article and she ruined it. She had changed it from an entertaining, instructive and useful story about how the company could reduce waste, helping their profits and the environment, to an article about a goddamn meeting. But since they were paying for it I had to write what they wanted. In articles like these the person with the least control over the content was the writer. I hated that.

To make matters worse, I was ashamed at myself. I was a professional writer and had secretly sabotaged a job because I didn't like how it was going. It would have been better to simply say no. I would have respected myself for standing up for my beliefs, but I had sacrificed my personal and professional integrity. And for what? A couple hundred tainted euros which I didn't even need.

This thought brought my musing to a stop. I was making more money than I needed, so why was I still doing this? Maybe it was time to stop writing what people told me to write and go back to writing what I wanted to write, like I had done with my books. Yes. This was exactly what I had been looking for, why I had been so unsatisfied and depressed. This was what was missing in my life. I had to write another book.

And, as it turned out, someone else had been thinking the exact same thing.

31

Tapio was my Swedish language tutor, but he was also my publisher. I had written two business books in English for him and he was constantly thinking of what I should write next. I was a weapon in his arsenal and he intended to make use of me. About every three months we would have a meeting and he would try to talk me into a book idea.

'I think a book about the Finnish gaming industry would be good,' he told me. 'There are lots of good stories there: Rovio, Supercell, Remedy.'

'Yeah, I guess so,' I said.

'You have contacts in the gaming industry so start talking to people and see what they think.'

'What about what I think? I want to write something else.'

'Like what?'

'I don't know yet.'

'You need to write something. Just go and talk to them. It can't hurt.'

So I did. The executives in the gaming industry were enthusiastic, of course, but not everyone was pleased to hear that I was exploring the idea. I set an appointment with Taloussanomat journalist Elina Lappalainen, and when we met she avoided my eyes and looked extremely uncomfortable. Elina took a deep breath and finally looked at me.

'We are competitors,' she said. 'I am also writing a book about the Finnish gaming industry and I will not speak to you.'

I blinked. 'Okay,' I said. I stood up and turned to leave.

'Normally I would talk to you,' she said hurriedly as I was walking away. 'But not now.'

I turned around and looked at her again. 'Okay,' I said again and left.

I went back to Tapio and told him what happened.

'I have doubts there is a market for one book about the Finnish gaming industry,' I admitted to him, 'much less two.'

'If it is a big enough story there are often several books written about it, just like what happened with Nokia.'

'But is this a big enough story?'

He didn't answer, which was an answer. Lappalainen's *Pelien valtakunta* never generated much interest, as far as I could tell, so I was relieved my instinct had been correct. I didn't want to only write for a marginal local audience. The problem was that I knew what I didn't want to write, but I didn't know what I did want to write.

At our next irregularly scheduled meeting to talk about book ideas Tapio suggested we focus on one big gaming company. I didn't have any excuses prepared and couldn't make up any on the spot, so I contacted Ilkka Paananen, who I had interviewed back when Supercell was still a startup squirming in the sea of gaming tadpoles. Yet things had changed quite a bit for him since those early days, and one of his assistants politely told me he wasn't interested in even discussing the idea.

Tapio dragged me to another company who were more welcoming. I sat in a few meetings and listened to their thoughts about a book. I didn't have anything to say because I didn't have any ideas for them. Yet soon rumours began to swirl about difficulties in the firm and they prudently decided now was not a good time for a writer to be poking his nose around. They ended our joint exploration with a letter which was strikingly similar in tone and wording to a job applicant rejection letter, which greatly amused Tapio and I.

I started working on a novel which interested me, at least to some extent. I was about a third of the way through when Tapio contacted me again. He was so excited about his next idea that he invited me to a nice restaurant for lunch.

'We need to write a book about Slush,' he told me.

Slush is the student-run organisation dedicated to entrepreneurship and startups in Finland. They have a conference at the beginning of every winter which draws thousands of people from around the world.

'I'm not interested in a book about Slush,' I said. 'I write a dozen articles about the event every year. I don't want to do a whole book.'

'Are you just going to write articles for the rest of your life?'

'No, I'm working on a novel.'

'How long have you been working on it?'

'Six months.'

'How many words do you have?'

'Maybe 15,000.'

'Is it any good? Tell me the truth.'

'No.'

'Do you have faith you can fix it?'

I hesitated.

'Look, it is perfectly fine to stop a project that isn't working out,' he said. 'Lots of authors do that. Try something else for a while, and then you can come back to your novel later. Besides, after your Nokia book it will be easy to sell this one. If we get the Slush organisation with us we could even sell the book at the event to a captive audience.'

I groaned. Tapio was right and I hated it.

'Okay, I'll do it, but on one condition,' I said. 'At some point I'm going to send you ten pages of something. I don't know what it is yet because I haven't figured it out myself. But once I have something, I want you to read those ten pages and tell me if you would keep reading or not. I don't want you to say anything else besides that. That's what I want from you.'

'Deal!'

I still wasn't a believer in the Slush book. This wasn't my idea; it wasn't my book. Then make it your book, a part of me said. Take Slush and make it your story. You're interested in entrepreneurs, technology and business narratives so this is perfect for you.

I began contacting people in the organisation. Most of the Slush executives are fiercely protective of everything Slush and would have nothing to do with me, but the Slush board are more open-minded and were intrigued. I had one meeting after another with people like Miki Kuusi, Timo Ahopelto and Jenny Gyllander, and they were all cautiously enthusiastic. I broadened my research and began talking to others, like Kai Lemmetty, who had been one of the founders of the movement but were no longer involved. They were also eager to talk, but perhaps for different reasons.

Out of the blue I received a message from Timo: they loved the idea so much they were going to steal it. Slush decided to write, produce and sell the book themselves. The organisation got most of their work done through student volunteers and he said they had decided to do the same thing with the book. I thought a book written by a committee of students would look like a book written by a committee of students, but I was polite enough not to mention that to him.

Quite soon word trickled through the publishing industry that Slush had instead wanted a native Finn to write the book. They eventually chose Tuomas Vimma, whose *Enkeleitä ja yksisarvisia* came out in late 2018. I don't know if the 'student writers' idea was an excuse to let me down gently or if they came to their senses and acknowledged they needed a professional but didn't want to come back to me.

Timo and I parted amiably enough, because I genuinely like

Timo and the Slush movement. He seems to still like me as well, and worked with me on a couple of other articles. I was also grateful because he gave me an excuse not to write something I couldn't force myself to be excited about. My publisher, on the other hand, was understandably outraged.

'That was my idea and they stole it,' Tapio fumed. 'Let's write a book about Slush without their involvement. Without the organisation's blessing we might sell less, but it will be a better book without them trying to influence the content. That was the formula we used with Nokia and it worked well.'

'Slush is one of my most profitable times of the year,' I countered. 'I write dozens of articles about the event and the companies there. I have been to every Slush except the first few. What if I piss them off and they blacklist me? I'll lose all those contacts, all those stories and all that income.'

I couldn't imagine Miki and Timo would actually blacklist me from their event, but it was a great excuse. Tapio was worried about the possibility and reluctantly backed down. He didn't want me to jeopardise my freelancing.

Back at my computer I read through my novel. It was shit and I didn't have any hope for it, at least at present. Tapio was right. I needed to ditch this and try something else. During a period of several weeks I wrote a list of ten different ideas and decided to write one page on each. Some of the pages were simply plot outlines, others were character synopsis and a few were hesitant first pages of narratives. But one was something different. Time disappeared and I was seven pages in before I snapped out of my nirvana writing trance. Okay, I thought, I have something here.

My phone beeped. Tapio wanted to meet the next day. This wasn't our normal Swedish meeting, so I knew he had another book idea.

'Peter Vesterbacka,' Tapio said before I had even sat down.

'He might be interesting,' I said carefully.

Peter was indeed an interesting fellow, having been involved with the beginning of Slush and the runaway success of Angry Birds. Now he wanted to build a tunnel under the Baltic Sea between Tallinn and Helsingfors. Peter claimed he would use nebulous Chinese technology and get it done in only five years for only fifteen billion euros. I thought his cost and time estimates were off by a factor of three, but maybe he could convince me otherwise.

'Do you know him?' Tapio asked.

'I don't really know him, but we run into each other occasionally. We say hi if we see each other somewhere, and I think he gave me a quote or two for different articles.'

'See if he would talk to us about it.'

I shot Peter a quick email and he was willing to talk, but this time I didn't follow up. When Tapio next asked me about Peter's book I unapologetically told him no.

'I can't. I have to write about someone else,' I said. 'Guess who.'

32

I checked the Tallinn-Helsingfors ferry schedule and looked at my clock. If it took Saga an hour to get disembarked, take a tram to Järnvägstorget, ride the metro to Drumsö and walk home, she should be opening her front door right about now.

It was still two hours from my regular quitting time, so I tried to continue working. I went back to the article I was writing and the letters on the screen were meaningless. I bounced my foot, looked out the window, scratched my neck, chewed my fingernails, and couldn't read the sentence I had just written without getting lost and having to start over. The only thing I could think of was what was in Saga's flat right now.

Finally I gave up and put my shoes on. I didn't run, but I walked very quickly to Saga's house. She let me in—she had never given me her spare key, and I had never given her mine—and I knew from the look on her face there was a problem.

'We didn't get any,' she said, and threw herself on her couch. 'He never showed up and his phone was disconnected.'

'Fuck!' I yelled in frustration. 'I really wanted some tonight.'

'It's not my fault! Why don't you fucking get some for once?'

'I'm the one who pays for it!'

'Big shit. I'll be the one who pays for it if we get caught.'

We fumed at each other for a moment and suddenly I had a memory. I was trying to go without any alcohol and at nine in the morning a craving hit me so hard I could barely withstand it. Yet I gritted my teeth and focused on the tiny bumps under the letters F and J on my keyboard, and within a few seconds the craving went away.

'Do you know what's happening?' I asked Saga. 'I'm addicted to Oxy. I wanted it so bad and when I couldn't get it I got angry. I'm glad you couldn't get any. We don't need it.'

'Jussi gave me two of his.'

She displayed a little baggy made for freezing berries. Inside were two little round pills, swallowed up in the expanse of clear plastic.

'Flush them,' I said.

'I'm not flushing them,' said Saga. 'If you want to stop, fine. But I'm not going to throw these away. We can finish these off and not get any more.'

I looked up from the pills to her face. Jussi gave her more than two pills, I realised with a sudden fury, but she doesn't want to tell me.

'No. This is just like the booze. If I have a bottle, I have to drink it. The only way to not take them is not to have them.'

'No one is forcing you to take them.'

She went into the kitchen, used a knife to break a pill in two and swallowed half of it with a toss of her head. Taking half was a sure sign that she had already taken one. She wetted a finger, used it to pick up a few stray pharmaceutical crumbs and licked them off. You don't waste a speck. I watched it all in morbid fascination.

Just one more. I imagined the relaxed euphoria which was right there. I could see it on her counter. Just take one more and then you're done. Promise yourself that you will never touch another. I didn't realise I was biting my lip until I stopped and felt the pain.

'Listen, I can't know about this,' I told her. 'Don't do it in front of me. Don't tell me about it. Please. If it isn't in front of me it is easier to handle. I can't take them anymore. They make me numb and foggy and I can't feel what I need to feel in order to write...in order to live. And I need to leave right now.'

'Suit yourself.'

Saga kicked back on the couch and gave me a lazy thumbs-up. It was already affecting her. I gave her a perfunctory kiss goodbye and hurried outside. After about thirty metres I realised I had stopped walking.

Just one more. Then you can stop. It's right there. Just one more.

I jerked myself into motion, stuck my hands in my pockets, lowered my face to the wind, and walked home.

My thoughts followed the rhythm of my steps: no, no, no.

33

'Boletus, or tatti in Finnish,' Robert said. 'This is the king of the mushrooms, and my favourite.'

He was already some way ahead, so I hurried to catch up.

For several months I had been spending more of my free time with Robert. I still went over to Saga's, but not as often because the craving for Oxy always hit hardest when I was at her place. She didn't seem to mind my absences.

I missed Saga, but I missed Minttu as well. For months every day had begun with sending morning greetings to each other. We told each other what we were doing, shared screen shots of the games we were playing or sent each other funny videos. The day finally ended with a 'good night' right before sleep. Yet those messages had suddenly stopped coming, and she rarely replied to the ones I sent.

I hadn't understood how important those messages were for me until they were gone. There was now a hole in my life. Over time our conversations, which used to be on the top of every messaging app, gradually dropped down the screen into digital oblivion. I couldn't keep up with her on social media because she now only used private accounts open only to her friends. I knew nothing about her life and missed her intently.

The boletus looked out of proportion to my generic idea of a mushroom, like what you found in a supermarket. The dirty white stem was thick and tall, and the brown cap seemed ludicrously small, not much larger in diameter than the stem.

Robert was helping me to delve further into Finnish nature. Picking mushrooms was supposedly an integral part of life in Finland, but I had never done it. Robert had accepted to be my mushroom tutor immediately.

'You break it off close to the ground and carve off the dirty bottom as if you're making a spear. Good, there's no worms. It will turn bluish when exposed to the air. Stick your tongue on it.'

I stuck my tongue on the cut stem. I tasted faint whiffs of cool earth, like a fading memory.

'Taste bitter?'

'No.'

'Then it's good. If it tastes bitter it is another variety of tatti which isn't good to eat.'

Robert was single-minded. He was there to find mushrooms and nothing else. He tore down paths at a brisk pace, searching for the right places. Sandy soil, hillsides, mixed forest, logging in past years...he called out signs to look for as he hurried along. When he came to a likely place he waved me ahead.

'I move a lot slower than you do,' I said. 'You're going to get impatient.'

'No, I won't,' he lied.

I lead for about thirty seconds, carefully looking to the left and right. The yellow chanterelles should have been easy to spot, but I was constantly tricked by fallen yellow birch leaves. If he saw some he told me to look again. If he didn't see anything he shot off in another direction or passed me on the faint animal trail to charge ahead.

'You should write a book about mushroom hunting for foreigners,' he said.

'There are already tons of mushroom books on the market.'

'Yes, but they aren't complete. They are always about how to identify different ones or prepare them. They leave unsaid things that Finns know, like the Everyman's Right and where to look for them.'

'How do you know where to look for them?'

'My wife and I do this every year. We're fanatical,' he said. 'So we know old places, but we are constantly looking for new ones. I'll look on Google Maps to find likely areas, and then we come out and scout. You can even hunt mushrooms as you drive down roads.'

'Maybe you can,' I said. 'I can't see them when they are right in front of me.'

'You're looking too hard. Just pass your eyes over an area and they will jump out at you. If you try to pick them out of the undergrowth you will never see them.'

As the day went on I became better, but I was still not as good as him. When he passed a few chanterelles without stopping I suspiciously asked him if he had left them for me to find. He claimed to have missed them, although I thought he might have been trying to boost my confidence.

'What is chanterelle in Swedish?' I asked.

'Kantarell, but they often use the nickname guld, gold, because of their colour,' Robert said. 'Why are you asking about Swedish?

'I'm trying to learn it.'

'What's wrong with Finnish?'

'To be honest, Finnish is a lot more difficult for me. Swedish is easier and I have a lot of Swedish-speaking acquaintances.'

'You're making a mistake.'

I thought of not being able to talk to Nea and was silent, and, unusually, so was he. He just waited, watching me.

'How's that?' I finally asked.

'People learn the language of the country they live in to communicate. How many people are you going to be able to talk to with Swedish? There are probably more people who speak English than Swedish in this country.'

'I need to speak an official language, and English isn't one of them.'

'Swedish has other problems. Swedish-speakers have too many rights as a preferred minority, like quotas in government jobs and universities. People are upset about it.'

'I like Swedish better,' I said. 'Finnish is shit.'

'If you get fluent in Swedish you aren't going to fit in,' Robert said, ignoring my insult. 'And you're picking it for the wrong reason anyway. A minority picking a minority language isn't going to make you any more at home in Finland.'

'Are you saying this because you work for a Swedish company? Is this some personal beef you have with Swedish speakers?'

'It's personal because I'm your friend,' he said. 'I'm a foreigner myself, you know, even though I have a Finnish parent and a Finnish passport. I didn't grow up in Finland, and that makes me a foreigner. When I speak about the Finnish language and immigrants I know what I'm talking about.'

'I tried to learn Finnish, but I can't! It's beyond me. But I'm not giving up on this fucking country yet so I'm putting my money on Swedish.'

'You always pick the dying. All your books are about dying companies or dying people. You could live anywhere in the world, like vibrant and exiting Asia, but you choose to live in the most tired and decrepit civilisation on the planet. Now you pick a language dying in this country. Swedish has been on life support for forty years.'

I calmed down and thought before answering.

'Everyone is interested in youth, growth, the next big thing,' I said slowly. 'No one cares about the end of that cycle: age and decay and the end of things. But there is beauty in the dying. They have grace and dignity. Growing things have hope, but dying things have soul. Maybe that is what attracts me. You're my friend, so you should understand this.'

When I finished he silently turned and walked back into the forest, slower this time, as if he was thinking. Two minutes into the woods Robert stopped again.

'Do you see anything?'

It took me a few moments, but I finally spotted a white mushroom half-hidden under yellow birch leaves.

'That's death cap, the most poisonous mushroom in Finland. If you eat one there will be nothing any doctor can do.'

I knelt down and looked at the mushroom closely. It had a pale yellowish-green cap with gills underneath and the remnants of a skirt around the off-white stem.

'Here's a trick to help you remember poisonous mushrooms,' Robert said with a grin in his voice. 'Avoid religion and women, meaning don't touch any mushroom with a steeple or a skirt. The steeple is a little point on the cap and the skirt is around the stem. Check every mushroom three times: once when you pick it, once when you clean and preserve it, and once when you prepare it. If at any stage you aren't completely positive that it is a good mushroom then throw it away.'

I had looked at him as he talked and then looked back at the death cap. It didn't have a steeple on the cap, but it did have a little skirt. It seemed so innocuous, just a quiet white mushroom on the forest floor among the pine needles, twigs and dead leaves.

'Don't even touch that,' Robert said strangely. 'You have a habit of messing with things people warn you against.'

I looked up at him and he was studying me with an odd expression. I stood up and signalled I was ready to go on, and after a moment of indecision he turned and led me deeper into the forest.

We came into a clearing on the side of a hill and something on the horizon caught my attention. It looked like a line of mountains at the edge of my eyesight. Clouds. These weren't normal clouds, the fluffy white ones which popped up on a summer day or the angry black ones which unleashed rain in the spring and autumn. No, these were the grey clouds of Finnish winter, massive, unmoving, implacable. They would cover the world like the concrete vault of a tomb for months. No sun, no stars, no moon, no blue sky. Nothing but the oppressive grey horror poised over us. The bad times were coming early this year.

34

Nea asked me to take her to a hobby horse competition. Kaarle and Mari were gone on some errand, and I had a painful suspicion that Nea had asked me to take her because she couldn't find any other ride.

Stop being stupid, I told myself on the drive over to their house. Nea really likes you.

Niilo and his babysitting cousin were absorbed in their video games, but at least the dogs were happy to see me. Nea smiled nervously and paced constantly.

'Are you excited?' I asked. 'This will be fun!'

Nea glanced at me in an exasperated appeal: don't make me speak English.

With Nea consumed with pre-competition jitters I played with the dogs and talked to the boys about their games. After chatting with them for about half an hour it was almost time to leave, but Minttu still hadn't come out of her room. I knocked on her door.

'Come in,' she said in English, knowing it was me.

I walked in and barely got a 'hello' out of my mouth before she shoved a book at me.

'Here's your book,' she said.

She handed me *The Hobbit.* I stood holding the book in my hands. She lay back on her bed, headphones on, staring at her phone.

'This was a gift to you,' I said. 'It's yours. You can keep it.'

'No, you take it back,' she said.

'You might want to read it again someday.'

'I don't want it anymore,' she said. 'It will only get ripped up here.'

She waved her arm angrily, taking in everyone and everything around her. She glanced at me and looked back at her phone. I wandered around her room with my rejected gift in my hand, looking at stuffed animals and jewellery and old pictures on the walls she had drawn.

'So what's going on?' I asked. 'I haven't talked to you in a long time.'

'Nothing is going on,' Minttu said.

'Have you been swimming or jumping on the trampoline with Niilo and Nea?'

'No, they're annoying.'

'Oh, come on. You must be doing something.'

'Today I wanted to go see…someone…but I can't so I just sit by myself.'

'Listen, kulta,' I said. 'Anytime you want to do something, you call me. We can go to Borgbacken or the zoo, or go shopping or see a movie. Or we could go to the ballet again, like the time I took you to see the Nutcracker. Anything you want, anytime you want. We haven't done anything together for ages.'

She smiled at me sadly and looked away. I realised: yes, she is lonely, but no, she doesn't want to spend time with me. Minttu was fourteen now, more interested in her friends than her old American pseudo uncle. My connection to her was tenuous at best, through a convoluted series of failed marriages. She should be spending time with her friends, not me. Maybe giving me back *The Hobbit* was her way of saying our old relationship was over.

'You know, I just started watching this video when you came in,' she said in frustration.

I looked at her. She looked at her phone.

'Okay,' I said. 'I'll leave you to your video.'

She didn't answer. I looked at her not looking at me and left her room, closing the door behind me.

I remembered once when I arrived at their house and lingered in the front yard to talk to Kaarle. Minttu had come to the door to greet me. I waved at her and continued talking, but her patience was gone in two seconds.

'Come *here*, David!' she had said, and I had abandoned Kaarle in the middle of a sentence to run to her.

Another time I was ending my visit and had already said goodbye to everyone. I was in the entryway, putting on my shoes and coat. The others had gone back to their separate activities, but Minttu alone had followed me to the door. When I was ready to leave I held my arms open to her for a second goodbye hug, and the look of pure delight and happiness on her face as she ran into my arms imprinted itself on my soul.

I remembered.

I remember.

35

On the wall of Saga's kitchen hung a small tapestry of *Maamme*, the Finnish national anthem. It was modern but had a venerable look to it. Perhaps it was a reproduction from how it appeared in the mid-19th Century, or perhaps it was what modern marketers think consumers wanted it to look like.

The scene had a stereotypical Finnish lake in the background, with a rocky isle and shores covered with trees. In the foreground were two birches framing the picture, with their stylised roots swirling down the bottom and joining.

In the lower-centre part of the tapestry were several verses. *Maamme*, *Vårt land*, *Our land.* I often stopped to puzzle over the strange words, translating what I could and asking Saga for help when I couldn't.

Oi mamme, Suomi, synnyinmaa,
Soi, sana kultainen!
Ei laaksoa, ei kukkulaa,
Ei vettä rantaa rakkaampaa,
Kuin kotimaa tää pohjoinen,
Maa kallis isien!

Our land, Finland, our land of birth
Sound, the golden word!
There's no valley, no hill
No water, shore more precious
Than this our northern homeland,
The dear land of our fathers!

'There's a big difference between Finland and America,' I said as I looked at the tapestry. 'Have you ever heard that old Arlo Guthrie song, *This land is your land*?'

Saga nodded.

'That song is about acceptance and sharing America. "This land is your land, this land is my land...this land was made for you and me". But *Maamme* is about exclusion. "Our land of birth...land of our fathers". If you aren't born Finnish this isn't your land.'

She looked at me over her cup of coffee and said nothing.

'This can never be my anthem even if I live in Finland fifty years and speak the language and have citizenship. Your country doesn't want me or anyone like me. Compare that to America.

"Give me your tired, your poor, your huddled masses yearning to breathe free".'

Saga sighed and put down her coffee.

'Doesn't your president want to build a wall to keep people out?' she asked.

'Trump is a joke. He'll never get it done. Americans might get grumpy, but they aren't filled with hate like he is.'

'Bullshit. America is defined by hate. Hate the Native Americans, hate the blacks, hate the Soviets, hate the poor, hate sexual minorities, now it is hate the immigrants. Trump is perfect for America,' she was remorseless. 'And wasn't *This land is your land* a protest song against injustice in American society? Just like *Born in the USA*? Americans turned them into patriotic drivel, pretending they were something they are not. That's America. You take shit and pretend it is a pot of gold. You claim the whole world is envious of your pot of shit. You've brainwashed yourself. If you tell yourself lies long enough you believe it. I'm surprised that you of all people are still falling for that, because you have seen the world and know that isn't true.'

I looked at the tapestry and thought for a moment.

'I know; you're right,' I said. 'The American Dream is largely a lie. But it is a good-natured lie. It's a white lie. It gives hope, and there is precious little of that in the world. America is a land of optimism. America encourages you to have faith in yourself.'

'Finland encourages you to have faith in others. You'll never be at home here until you learn that,' Saga said. 'After your divorce why didn't you go back to the States?'

'That's a tough question, one that I've been trying to answer myself. At first I couldn't afford a plane ticket. Then I thought I could find what I was looking for here.'

'Did you find it?'

'I'm still looking.'

36

Saga and I were spooning, but I couldn't get comfortable. I kept shifting around, to her annoyed grunts. I looked at her bookcase. All my books were in a row. She had read every one, complementing where they should be complemented and criticising where they should be criticised. Heljä had never read any of them, which was probably a good thing, because she had been in them. Only one person had noticed her in my books, my old friend Fran Weaver, and he was dead now. Cancer had killed him.

'What's wrong?' Saga asked.

'I'm not happy.'

'Keep going. Why aren't you happy?'

'I don't know. It's nothing, or maybe it is everything. I'm upset about the kids. Kaarle isn't entirely pleased with me having close relationships with them. And he's right, of course. I'm not a family member. I shouldn't be close to them, but I want to be. The kids themselves are growing away from me. Minttu is a teenager and doesn't care about me anymore. Nea can't speak English so we can't communicate. And Niilo is still so young.'

It was odd talking to her about them. I had never told Kaarle and his family anything about Saga. The closest I had ever come was with Minttu, when I casually mentioned something I learned about baking from 'my girlfriend.' Minttu had looked at me curiously but didn't pursue the topic. I didn't know if she had told her parents or not.

I wasn't trying to hide our relationship, but I also wasn't advertising it. If anyone asked if I was seeing someone I said yes, but few people ever asked. I was fearful that if Kaarle and Mari knew about Saga they would stop inviting me to their family events, like what happened when I was married. What would be even worse was if Kaarle and Mari felt obligated to invite both of us, and I would feel obligated to sit with the adults and drink coffee instead of jumping on the trampoline with Nea or having one of those long private conversations with Minttu which I loved so much.

'It sounds like they consider you as a family member,' Saga said. 'They even invite you to celebrate Christmas with them.'

'At least someone invited me,' I said. 'You didn't.'

'So this is what you are unhappy about. Us.'

'It's not just this,' I said, not wanting to explore this with Saga. 'Why am I in Finland anyway? I came here for a woman, but now I have no reason to be here. I can't even speak the language. I pretend like learning Swedish will finally make me feel at home here, but that's just a lie which everybody sees through, including me.

'It's also my work. It's good money, but I'm tired of it. I spend so much time and energy on nothing, articles about corporate crap or a bullshit topic the government wants to promote this quarter. Stories about automated accounting software, or how Finland was among the first countries in the world to give women full political rights.'

'Equality is important.' Saga's voice was cold.

'Yes, it is. It is an important story which we should tell the world. But it isn't *my* story. Don't you understand? All my creativity is being leeched out of me to promote keywords picked by overpriced consultants who study overpriced algorithms. It's like concentrating all your effort on blowing into a tornado. It's useless and your breath is gone in an instant. I want to write something meaningful to me and other human beings instead of fucking Google Trends.'

'So write another book,' she said.

'I can't! That is worst of all. I have to write but I can't. It's fucking torture. There's something wrong with me and I don't know what it is.'

Saga sat up and looked at me.

'Come to Jyväskyla with me for Christmas. In fact, come with me this weekend,' she said. 'I love you.'

I laid there, smelling her scent on the pillow and staring at my books. This was the first time either of us had said the L-word. Two paths lay before me. I remembered a similar situation several years before, when my wife was in bed and I sat on the couch in the darkness, thinking about our marriage, which by that point was in its agonal breaths. For a number of years I had known that I did not like my wife, but that moment I admitted that I did not love her, either. I had to make a decision. Should I euthanize our marriage or let it die on its own. I chose the latter because I didn't have the courage to do otherwise. Now I had another decision to make, and I wasn't going to make the same mistake again.

'Listen,' I said. 'Sometimes you aren't going to be my priority. Sometimes I'll want to do things with the kids and not you. Sometimes my writing is more important to me than anything, including you. I don't like it and I can't help it. It is just the way I am.'

Saga scooted across the bed away from me and wrapped her blanket around herself. I looked from my books to her. It was the first time I ever saw her vulnerable.

'No,' I said. 'No, don't love me.'

She gave me a long look.

'You're going to be very lonely,' she said.

'I already am.'

37

For the third year in a row Kaarle and Mari invited me to spend Christmas with them, and after several long hours staring out of my window at the dead trees and dead world I said yes. I did not believe Saga would repeat her invitation and she met my expectations.

Forcing my way into the front door with giant Landseers bounding with unsuppressed excitement was a challenge. I had to hold them at bay with one hand and take off my snowy shoes with the other. Kaarle, Mari and the older kids were busy with last minute preparations, but Niilo greeted me when I got through the dogs. The entryway was filled with bags and boxes of things they would be taking with them to Mari's parents' house. A few items were set apart, as if they were too important to be classed with the presents and food. I stopped and stared at them.

'It is starting to get really annoying doing that every night,' said Niilo.

I looked at him and back to the items. They were his irrigation bags, tubing, cone tip, plastic sleeves and lubrication, set apart as special. This was how the little boy had to manage his digestive tract after his colostomy.

'How long will you have to do that?' I asked him.

'All my life.'

'You do it every day? How long does it take?'

'It takes an hour. I do it at seven at night during school nights, and at eight at night on weekends.'

Niilo thought it was annoying now, when he was ten years old. What would it be like when he was out partying all night with his buddies and needed to do it? What would it be like in the shower with other boys after gym class? What about when he got naked with his first girlfriend? I wish I had some profound wisdom, a quote from Plato or Shakespeare to say to him, something which would put it all into perspective, something which would cheer him up and give him optimism for the future, but I had nothing.

Kaarle disrupted my solemn meditation on living with a colostomy and invited me into the kitchen for a cup of coffee. Kaarle and Mari always followed the Finnish custom with visitors and offered me coffee. We were close, but this ritual reminded us all that I wasn't one of them.

As we made small talk Minttu came and sat next to me. In her hands was a folder which I recognised. She patiently waited, and when a break came in the conversation I turned to her.

'Long time no see, stranger,' I said to her. 'Is that your end-of-term report card?'

She nodded and handed me the folder. I pulled out the paper with her grades.

'How many goddamn tens are there?' I asked, and Kaarle and Mari laughed.

'All of our kids are good at school,' Kaarle said. 'Minttu did very well.'

Indeed she did. I made Minttu explain each grade, even the ones I could translate. She had gotten the best possible score—ten—in about half of her courses. Math, chemistry, biology and home economics were tens. Nines in history and physical education. Her worst grades were eights in Swedish and Finnish.

'How did you only get a nine in English?' I asked her. 'You're fluent in English! I could drop you off alone in Kansas City or Manchester and you could talk to anyone you meet!'

'The grade is more than just knowing English,' Minttu said. 'It includes class participation and things like that.'

'You've really helped her with her English,' Kaarle said.

'Sometimes when Minttu speaks I hear myself. She uses some of my phrases and some of her words have an American accent to them, which is pretty unusual in Finland where a British pronunciation is more common. She must have picked up my mannerisms.'

Minttu was surprised at this. She hadn't realised that I had influenced her English that much, but Kaarle and Mari were smiling. They had noticed it, too.

'What is this one where you got a ten?' I asked.

Minttu frowned as she sought to explain. 'That is how you behave in school.'

'Ah! That was called "citizenship" when I was young. Maybe it still is,' I said. 'What is your average grade for all your classes?'

'Nine point three. Only one person in my class was higher.'

'Minttu, these grades are fantastic,' I told her. 'You worked hard for this and I am really proud of you.'

Minttu's face was so bright it could have blinded anyone who looked into it. This is what she lived for: meeting and exceeding the expectations of the adults around her.

'I'm proud of you too,' Kaarle said hurriedly.

That was odd, I thought. Undoubtedly Kaarle had told Minttu how happy he was with her academic performance, but he must have neglected to tell her the most important thing: how proud he was of her. At least I had told her, if her father didn't. Kaarle's sudden declaration was somewhat embarrassing and more than a bit sad. He had even used English so I would understand. She was the one who needed to hear this, not me. He should know his daughter better.

The only grade which somewhat disappointed me was 'citizenship'. Minttu constantly worked to satisfy adults like her teachers and parents. She never showed a hint of rebellion, a sign that she was experimenting with her independence. The only time I had ever seen her rebel was when she wanted me to pick her up and Kaarle had said no. She had waited until he wasn't around to disobey him. Besides that, she was like an automaton, only doing what adults wanted her to do. A bit of rebellion would be good for her.

Nea appeared.

'David, come see my new game Star Stable!' she yelled. 'It has horses!'

'David, come watch me on Minecraft!' Niilo called.

I gave Minttu's shoulder a squeeze and followed Niilo and Nea. Through the window I saw Mari leave with her parents to grab something at the store they had forgotten. Nea and Niilo were in full sibling rivalry mode, fighting for my attention.

'That's a cool diamond sword, Niilo,' I told him. 'How do you make the horse jump?' I asked Nea.

There was a bang in the hallway. I stood upright from where I had been watching Niilo play over his shoulder. Minttu was digging through a drawer and throwing things on the floor, scarves, old phone chargers, gloves. Crash. Minttu slammed an old calendar down. It flopped open to reveal Toukokuu 2015 with incomprehensible scribbles on various days like the arcane babblings of the sybil.

'Just a second,' I told Nea and Niilo, and went out to Minttu. 'Whoa, whoa, kulta. What's going on?'

She stumbled over the English words, something which she did only on those rare occasions when she was really upset.

'Mom asked me to get her…her…gloves and I can't find them!'

I stepped over piles of things and glanced at a few gloves she had already found and rejected as not being the right ones.

'What are they?'

'Black leather.'

'I'll help you find them.'

She was digging through the drawers so I checked on top of the cabinet.

'They aren't there,' she snapped. 'Mom said they were in the drawer.'

'Well, if you can't find them in the drawer they must not be there. Don't worry; we'll find them.'

I checked other likely places someone would leave gloves: on the kitchen table, next to the door when you walk inside, coat pockets—but Niilo and Nea were frantic. We would be leaving within minutes and here I was wasting time looking for their mother's gloves instead of sharing their favourite video games.

I was at a loss where to find the gloves, so gave up and went to the doorway of the bedroom. Here I could see what Niilo and Nea had to show me while simultaneously keeping a sympathetic eye on Minttu. This was the drawback of her being mature, trusted and dependable. When someone needed something they always asked Minttu, and this could get frustrating. Suddenly I noticed tears in her eyes. I had never seen her cry before and had no idea what to do. I stood there frozen, completely impotent.

Kaarle strolled into the hallway, fists on hips, casually asked about the commotion, received Minttu's answer, and folded his daughter into his arms, whispering soothing, mysterious Finnish words. She calmed immediately and clung to him.

Checkmate.

My mouth did not pop open, but my mind did. It was a revelation, and I watched in awe and not a little jealousy. That could have been me, calming and soothing her and making her feel better, but I hadn't understood her.

When Minttu was upset I had hurried to her. I believed the problem was a lost pair of gloves, so I had tried to logically fix the problem by helping her find them. Kaarle was different. He focused on his daughter. Where I saw missing gloves Kaarle saw his upset little girl. I had been so smug after the incident with the report card, and imagined that she needed to show a bit of rebellion and independence. I had thought that I understood Minttu better than her father, but I had been spectacularly wrong. I didn't know a goddamn thing about her.

There would be times in Minttu's life when she would be upset by things which had no logical solution. Bullies at school. Dick boyfriends. Illnesses. Incompetent bosses. What could I offer her then? Nothing.

This was why Kaarle was the beloved empathetic father, intimately bound up in the lives of his kids, while I was the fun pseudo-uncle who came every few weeks to play games and give them expensive presents. If Minttu wanted someone to splurge on her back-to-school shopping she might condescend to come to me, but if she needed a shoulder to cry on she would run to him. Every time. 'My Minttu' was what I endearingly called her, but that was a monumental lie. She was, is, and always will be Daddy's Girl.

I had thought that I was part of their lives, and I was, but only superficially. At that moment I realised how unimportant I was. If I were to disappear their lives would not change in any meaningful way. I was absolutely nothing important to them.

My existence is not necessary.

38

Mari and her parents returned from the store and we were ready to leave. Her father would drive one car while Kaarle drove another. A brief discussion ensued on who would ride with whom. I chose Mari's dad and slid into the backseat. Out of the foggy window I saw Minttu climb in with Kaarle, as did Mari and Nea. Niilo and his grandmother joined me with Mari's dad. The long drive up to Mari's parents new house was quiet. Niilo played on his phone and I stared out the window at the grey snow and bare trees.

Mari had a large extended family, and there were too many of us to eat together at the kitchen table. Most of the adults sat at the table, but Kaarle ate on the couch with Minttu on one side and Nea and her cousin Elina on the other.

After dinner it was time to open gifts. Mari's mother gave me chocolate and Kaarle and Mari gave me a cookbook. I sat on the couch and watched the kids open my gifts: Minttu got a scarf, Nea a sweatshirt and Niilo a Roblox gift card. I had chosen modest things for once, which didn't go unnoticed.

'What did you get Minttu?' Kaarle asked me.

'A scarf.'

He digested this for a moment.

'Just a scarf?'

I nodded and he said no more.

The only person who had asked me what I wanted for a Christmas gift was Nea and I told her to draw me something. She presented me with a yellow folder tied with a lace pink ribbon tied in a big bow. Inside were about ten drawings, some of me which she had copied from photos on Instagram, and some of her own design. She had three variations of I Love You! with hearts pierced by arrows. I sat and stared at them a long time, and Kaarle stared at them too.

'Damn, this took a lot of effort,' I said. 'How long did this take her?'

'I don't know,' said Kaarle. 'I didn't even know she made them.'

Mari was watching with a big grin on her face. She had known.

'Pidätkö?' Mari asked.

'Yes. I like them very much.'

I called Nea away from her cousin Elina to sit beside me and hugged her close for a long time. She normally enjoyed hugs, but now she was restless. She wanted to go back to Elina.

'Okay, I'll let you go,' I told her. 'I just wanted to thank you very much for your drawings. These are some of the nicest gifts I have ever received.'

Finally, reluctantly, I let Nea go to play with her cousin. Niilo was absorbed in a video game with other cousins. Minttu ignored me completely. For the first time since I had known her she hadn't sat next to me at dinner. She had neither thanked me for her gift nor had given me one. Her scarf was her favourite colour pink, and it was also under a pile of empty boxes at her feet. She didn't even look at me. On this occasion she was glued to her father. She had rode in the car with him, ate with him, talked to him. Kaarle leaned back on the couch, his arms outstretched on the back, and she—who disliked all public signs of affection—sat down and snuggled against him.

You win, Kaarle, as you should.

I got up and went to the kitchen to sit down by myself. I held an uneaten Christmas star pastry in my hand and looked out of the window at the bare birch branches moving in the breeze under the grey Finnish sky. I remembered the feelings of another Christmas, another kitchen, another Christmas star.

Mari's mother came in to get a cup of coffee. She was short, chubby and jolly, like a Christmas elf. She also didn't speak a word of English. She babbled something and pointed at Nea's folder in my hand. I gave it to her and watched as she made embellished gasps to show me how impressed she was with the drawings.

'Missä on Nea?' she asked.

'Med Elina.'

'Missä Minttu?'

'Med Kaarle.'

She made an exaggerated show of surprise and frowned. I tried to smile at her. Everyone knew that they were my girls, or used to be, and she had probably never seen me before without one or the other at my side.

'Ah. Miksi olet yksin?'

'Because I'm an outsider.'

She blinked, smiled and turned away, what everyone does when they don't understand your language.

39

I hadn't been home to America in five years. For a long time my excuse was the expense, and when that was no longer viable my excuse was that I didn't want prying questions about my next book or my post-divorce life. Then one day soon after Christmas my sister Ann sent me a message about taking my eighty-six-year-old mother to the heart doctor and a desire to see Mom again—to see home again—surged up so strong that I immediately went online and bought plane tickets.

Once upon a time I was proud to hold an American passport travelling around the world, but I had a vague disquiet about it nowadays. I kept the passport in my pocket and only pulled it out when necessary. The immigration official in Chicago was as friendly as the stereotypical American, asking about my last name and if I was related to the famous E.L. Cord who built Cord automobiles in the 1930s. I said I wasn't and he was mildly disappointed.

On the approach into Indianapolis I stared out of the window, hoping to catch a glimpse of the Indianapolis Motor Speedway where I had watched Mika Häkkinen win his last race. I was on the wrong side of the plane, but I did get to see an enormous change around the airport. They had an entirely new entrance off the interstate, and the vast green fields of the airport had been replaced by a massive solar park.

I was surprised and baffled to see the solar panels. Indiana was one of the most conservative states in the Union, one of those places where they wanted to open up national parks for oil drilling and believed in clean coal. But it had been a long time since I'd been in America. Maybe things had changed.

Ann picked me up and insisted on driving through our little town Versailles (pronounced Vur-sales in true Hoosier fashion) so I could see all the changes. New court house, new streets, new buildings. It was like visiting a strange town instead of the one I had grown up in. I tried to imagine where my friends and I had hung out, but it was all gone, all obliterated.

The family farm was also changed. This is where I had lived in my youth, only coming inside occasionally to sleep. The old woods had been logged and it looked like the battlefield of Verdun a few years after the war. I had known every tree, every bush and every dry creek bed, but now I couldn't recognise a thing. The little saplings which had been growing in fence rows were now towering things, a line of green behemoths. I stood out in the field behind Mom's house and stared and wondered what the hell had happened.

Mom hadn't changed, though. She seemed a bit shrunken but was as spry as ever. When she noticed a burned-out lightbulb she hopped up on a chair to change it like someone aged twelve, not close to ninety. In the refrigerator she had prepared all of my favourite foods: meatloaf, Hoosier-style chili, venison supplied by my brother. She even had her home-made white bread, which was how I got my love of baking. On the counter was a pile of Reese's peanut butter cups. When I had first moved to Finland they had been hard to find as rare imports, and Mom had remembered me saying how much I missed them.

Mom gave me a long soliloquy of her daily life and all the

things my brother and sister did for her. Wayne cut her grass and gave her a car, which he always kept serviced and full of fuel. Ann took care of the house and shopping and stopped by every day to say hello.

'I don't know what I would do without my children,' she said, and the pain was so bad I couldn't breathe.

Neighbours and relatives appeared out of nowhere. Prodigal son, etc. People asked about the divorce, were amazed at how long my hair was, talked about reading my books and asked what I was writing now.

'I'm superstitious about my writing,' I said. 'I don't like to talk about it until it is finished.'

Everyone nodded and smiled in understanding. A writer is supposed to be eccentric.

The weather was glorious, about 15 degrees and sunny. I kept excusing myself from Mom's kitchen to stand out on her patio and stare at the green grass, budding trees and the scattered pure white clouds sliding along the azure sky. People seemed amused that I kept remarking on the weather.

'I haven't seen stars or blue sky in three months,' I explained. 'Helsinki is covered by clouds from early autumn to mid-winter.'

They looked at each other with wide eyes and wide mouths, wondering how human life could exist in that nightmare which was the world outside America.

Through it all Ann was there. She was how Minttu had once been, my hostess, my friend, making sure I could always find what I wanted and that I would never sit alone. I was the stranger in Finland and needed Minttu. Now I was the stranger in America and needed Ann.

The first person I wanted to see was my brother Wayne. Mom let me use her car and Ann reminded me of the best route to take. Wayne lived about fifteen minutes from Mom's, on a heavily wooded farm in a river valley.

'Don't they have barbers in Finland?' were his first words.

'They're all on strike. Lousy socialists,' I said, giving him a hug.

We wandered around his property, looking at his chicken coop and garden. Wayne invited me to hop on the ATV with him and ride up the big hill behind his house. On top was a large grassy field where he stopped and pointed to paths the deer used and where the best blackberry bushes grew. Nestled back in the trees was a firepit and little camper where he hung out. We kicked back and listened to the wind in the trees.

'The ash trees here have some sort of disease,' Wayne said, pointing to one. 'It is spreading across the state and eventually most of them will die.'

'The maple trees in Finland are diseased,' I said. 'They get big black spots on their leaves late in the year.'

'Have you ever thought of moving back?' he asked.

'Yes.'

'Well, I got a couple of houses and I might be able to rent one to you. They have tenants now but I could see what I could do.'

I didn't answer.

The sky clouded over and began to spit rain. We rode back down the hill and went into his big freestanding garage, more like a barn, so he could show me his Model A. After admiring the antique Ford I sat down and turned my attention to all the things hanging on the walls: deer antlers, balloons from ancient celebrations, dart boards, the old Cord Oil Co. sign I had given him for Christmas when the world was young.

'That's a giant Trump flag,' I noted.

'He may have not been my first choice, but he is the only chance we have now to save America,' Wayne said, his voice getting louder as he went. 'And fucking Obama! But, no, don't get me started.'

I sat quietly. Wayne had softened as he grew older, but that old anger was still there and could burst out with provocation. I was still scared of him, but I had always looked up to him and admired him. He had a strong set of personal morals and ethics which were humanistic in nature but tempered by his Catholic upbringing. Wayne was the person I most wanted approval from. I had even written an essay about this on my college application when I was seventeen years old. I had thought the essay would remain secret with only the admissions officers, but they had mentioned it in my acceptance letter, bringing a half-hurt, half-proud comment from my father. Wayne was Dad's favourite, but Dad wanted to be mine.

I didn't dare tell Wayne that I didn't like Trump. I was afraid of him getting angry at me, yes, but I was more worried that he would be disappointed in me. I thought I could handle his anger; I knew I couldn't bear his disappointment.

40

My old friends Cindy and Jim threw a party for me, and all of the old crew came. It was fantastic. The beer and joking insults and old stories and sexual innuendo and howls of laughter filled the air. All of us had known each other since grade school and there were no secrets or shame. We had gone through everything together, from spelling tests to orgies.

There was much talk about my hair and my books. Matt was curious about something else, and as soon as he started talking everyone fell silent. Evidently this had been an object of curiosity and private discussion.

'I've noticed some of your Facebook posts disrespecting President Donald Trump. Are you still an American citizen?' Matt asked me.

'Yes, I'm an American citizen.'

'Are you still a Republican?'

'Yes, I consider myself a Republican. You know, you can be a Republican and not like Trump. He won a plurality of votes in the primary, but the majority of Republicans voted against him!'

I tried to explain why I didn't like Trump, how he was racist, lied, alienated America's allies, cozied up with dictators, made terrible budget decisions, took human rights from sexual and gender minorities, couldn't control his own administration, drove wedges in American society, rolled back environmental protections, promoted wealth inequality, decimated free trade... but I didn't even get the first word out. Cindy, being the good hostess she is, distracted everyone by immediately telling a dirty joke in her loud and piercing voice.

Later all the guys wandered out into the yard to pass around a bottle, leaving the women in the house. Lori appeared in the doorway.

'David, come inside!' she called urgently.

When I returned to the house all the women eyed me worryingly. Some of them had more than a bit of sympathy for my anti-Trump position and had decided not to leave me alone with the men, who were all radical Trumpists. This was a fun reunion, not a political debate.

'It's okay; we were just drinking some of Dale's rockgut Kentucky whisky and laughing about old times,' I reassured them.

'We have whisky in here,' Cindy said, handing me a bottle.

41

When the night began to get old I hopped in my best friend Chris's truck and we drove to his house. He had built a mancave in his basement. Steelers and Yankees signs hung on the walls. A record player and large collection of vintage vinyl—all classic rock which we loved—sat in the corner.

He had a fully stocked bar and an old whisky barrel made into a table. He turned on the television to replay a Yankees game from last season as I picked out a record, Led Zeppelin III.

We sat at the barrel-table and continued drinking.

'Do you remember that time we were camping and Dale got so drunk he didn't know where he was?' I asked. 'He climbed in my sleeping bag and I couldn't get him out. Then he started laughing and puking at the same time.'

'Oh, I don't think you've heard this story,' Chris said. 'A couple of years ago we were camping and Dale was drinking some weird tequila shit. I warned him it was hard stuff but he's dumber than a retarded bullfrog and guzzled it. He sat next to the fire and started puking and making the funniest ah-ah-ah noises I ever heard. It was like a gagging, asthmatic pug. I swear it was one of the top three funniest things I've ever seen.'

Chris was laughing at the memory but my smile was pained. I would have been there if I hadn't moved to Finland. I would have seen it, experienced it, would have laughed at the memory for years. These relationships, these experiences, I had all given up.

We fell silent for a moment and watched the Yankees. I had used to love the team but now I didn't recognise a single player. Now I watched European sports, football and Formula 1 and long-distance skiing.

I should have stayed quiet. I should have just watched the game and laughed about old times and drank my whisky. But I couldn't. I spoke and suffered the consequences.

'Politically motivated mass killings is not a sign of a healthy society,' I said. 'Trump is a symptom of this hate in America; he isn't the cause of it.'

'Those people were radicalised before Trump, but you won't hear it from the mainstream media. It doesn't fit your bullshit narrative.'

The familiar friendliness in Chris's eyes had changed to belligerence, and I felt anger surge up in me as well.

'I just said Trump was a symptom, not the cause. So stop trying to twist my narrative into whatever you are trying to do,' I said. 'We've been friends way too long for you to fuck with me.'

'I'm not trying to do anything you pencil necked cocksucker. Fuck you.'

42

I had come to America with the hopeful idea that maybe it was time to move back, but within a few days I realised America was no longer home for me. Everything had changed. The people, the places, the politics. I had changed too. I had experienced life in a country which believed education and health care were human rights and was prepared to raise taxes for them. I knew what it was like to live next to a country which was larger, stronger and a bully.

I was sure the president after Trump would be a 'normal' president who followed all the old rules of civility and respect, but the real worry was the succeeding president. A competent person in power who had learned from Trump's ability to stir up hate would be a terrible thing. I didn't want to be there to see it.

My time in Finland had shown me what it was like to be the other, to be the one who did not fit in and did not belong. Strangely, I was more attracted to that now. I was an outsider and would rather be in the minority than in the majority. I was ready to go back to Finland. The only problem was that I couldn't make a home there either.

43

I didn't wait to unpack or even change my clothes; I simply hurried down to Saga's still stinking of sweat and stale airplane air. I had been wrong. I did need her. I would make her a priority. I did love her, and I wanted her to love me. It was dark and drizzly and the street lights shined on the wet asphalt. I rang her bell and waited.

'Ja?' It was a man's voice.

I stared at the intercom and didn't answer. After a long wait I walked into the yard and sat down at a freezing cold and wet picnic table. The lights in her kitchen were on. The top of her head came into view for a brief instant and disappeared. Her bedroom blinds were down but light suddenly appeared around their edges. After a few minutes the lights went out. I still sat and watched and waited.

An eternity later the lights in her bedroom came on again. A minute later a man appeared in the kitchen, opening the refrigerator door. He was tall and skinny. Saga appeared beside him, leaning in to get something out of the refrigerator. She brushed against him and he leaned against her. He was talking animatedly and he followed her away from the window. It was Jussi, the once and current boyfriend.

I got up, felt my cold and wet ass, and walked home.

44

I was half drunk most of the time. I was becoming an expert at only drinking enough to be numb but not so much as to be unable to function. It started right after my morning shower and ended a few hours before bed. Sometimes I stared blearily at the computer. Sometimes I stared blearily out the window at the dead trees and mud. Sometimes I slept for eighteen hours.

One day at noon my phone beeped. It was an SMS from Nea.

'I got tickets to a hockey game!' she wrote. 'Will you take me tonight?'

I was so excited and happy that my fingers fumbled on the keys.

'Od...of ciurse sweeti...'

I stopped and stared at the screen. What the holy fuck was I thinking? I was going to drive drunk with little Nea in the car?

But I wanted to see her so bad. I missed her so much that it was a physical pain. I wouldn't have to drive for another three or four hours. I would be sober enough by then.

No, no, no. This was the stupidest motherfucking thing I have ever considered. Never, ever would I put Nea in danger. Besides, I would rather finish my whisky.

'I'm sorry, sweetie, but I have an appointment tonight,' I lied.

'Okay. I'm sad. Bye.'

Suddenly the realisation of the choice I had made was clear, and I gaped at myself in horror. I slammed my fist on my leg in a rage. I liked the pain, so did it again and again. I needed to see someone so badly, and Nea wanted to be with me. She was so cute, so pure, so loving, that my face was permanently in a smile when I was with her. But I had fucked it up. Alcohol had become more important than her.

No. Fucking. More.

I limped into the kitchen, pulled my bottle of whisky out of the cabinet and emptied it into the sink. An urge to drink the last drop hit me and I was so furious that I charged out onto the balcony, struggled to open the big glass pane, and threw the bottle out onto the brown dead grass. Instead of shattering dramatically it plopped impotently onto the soft ground. Eventually my laboured gasps of the cold air calmed me down.

Will I never be happy again?

45

I wasn't able to function. I couldn't write, I couldn't think, I couldn't work. I stewed in my loneliness. I had lost Saga, lost Chris and was probably losing the kids. I didn't have too many people left to lose. This was worse than the divorce. There I had only lost a wife, but now I had lost a girlfriend, a best friend and the closest things to family members I had in this grey hell of a country.

All of my life I had immersed myself in the worlds given to me by books, but now the only thing I could read was Kurt Vonnegut's *Slaughterhouse Five*. Vonnegut was also a native of Indianapolis who had a life-changing experience in Europe. I read it over and over again because I could relate to the main character Billy Pilgrim. He was a tortured soul and had come unstuck in time. He knew the hour of his death and made no attempt to avoid it.

I couldn't stand it any longer. I had to spend time with another human being. For the first time in months I reached out to that person who had done so much for me simply by being my friend. I would use bribery if I had to.

'Would you like to go shopping tomorrow?' I messaged Minttu. 'Your birthday is coming and I'll get you something.'

'No, I'm doing something Saturday.'

I had expected to be rejected, but it still hurt. I was on the verge of closing the messaging app but I saw she was typing.

'But we could go Sunday. Pick me up after two.'

I slept soundly for the first time in ages. For once I didn't even need to take a sleeping pill.

The dogs were the only ones to greet me at the door. Alone, I untied and took off my shoes. Finns always wore shoes that were easy to slip on and slip off, but not me. I picked shoes with laces. Kaarle and Niilo were playing games on their computers. Neither of them raised their eyes from their screens to glance at me. Mari was banging around in the kitchen, but she gave me a perfunctory smile. You are always politer to people you can't communicate with.

I didn't bother to say hello to anyone or waste time with small talk. I pushed the dogs out of the way and went back to the bedrooms. Minttu was on her phone and Nea was on her computer.

'Are you ready to go?' I asked Minttu.

She blinked in surprise at my hurry and hopped up.

'Okay,' she said.

Nea asked her something, her eyes still on her computer screen, and Minttu answered. I didn't wait but immediately went back to the front door to begin putting on my shoes.

'I want to go!'

Nea stood in the hallway smiling at me. I returned my attention to my shoelaces.

'No,' I said to my shoes. 'I can't talk to you. I need to talk to someone and you never bothered to learn English.'

There was silence until I heard Minttu's footsteps approaching.

'Nea's crying!' she suddenly said.

I looked up to see Nea hugging herself, face down, tears rolling down her cheeks.

'*Why do you hurt me?*' she shrieked.

This was not Nea's faux outrage at her siblings or pretend tears for attention. This was real pain, and it was like a siren going off in the house. Mari ran into the hallway. Kaarle abandoned his game to come, as did Niilo.

I snatched Nea away from them into a tight hug.

'I'm so sorry, Nea!' I told her. 'I haven't been feeling good. I'm really sad and not thinking straight. You know I like to spend time with you. Today it is Minttu, but you and I should do something next. How about we go to the activity park in Vanda? You love that place! Please don't cry. I'm really sorry.'

I was babbling. Nea could only understand bits and pieces of what I was saying, but she understood the hug and my tone of voice. She nodded against my chest, still sniffling. Mari firmly took her away from me and spoke loudly and encouragingly, cheering her up in their own language.

Niilo watched Nea with a strangely mature expression of compassion, but Kaarle slowly turned his face to mine. He had watched me spoil and dote upon his kids for years and the idea that I would hurt one had been completely incomprehensible. Now I could see the thought process behind his eyes: I would, in fact, hurt them, and now he needed to process this new information.

I looked to Minttu for support but her eyes were flicking constantly, touching everything but seeing nothing. Her face was glowing and there was an abstracted half-smile on her face. Minttu knew what was happening but it didn't affect her; she was completely consumed with something else going on in her head.

'Come on,' I muttered to her, snapping her back to the present. 'Let's go.'

46

Minttu hadn't even gotten her seatbelt fastened before she was talking. The incident with Nea completely dismissed, she told me what she was watching on Netflix, what she was building on Minecraft, the meals she had made, what was going on at school and the things she had done with her friends recently, all in one uninterrupted flow.

Minttu was always more outgoing when we were alone. In recent months she had tended to either ignore me or outright dislike me, but now that she was alone in my car she was talking like she was catching up with her best friend who she hadn't seen in ages. She poured herself out to me, her likes, dislikes, hopes, fears, dreams, experiences. This was like the old times, back when we had messaged each other every day. I hadn't expected this and the distress over what I had done to Nea subsided as Minttu talked. But suddenly I snapped to attention.

'When you come to my birthday party you're going to meet my boyfriend,' she was saying.

'Oh?'

'Yeah, Mom says its time he meets the rest of the family. She has been bugging me and bugging me about it.'

This is why she is so abstracted, I realised. She can't stop thinking about him. I asked the normal questions: his name, his age, his school, where he lived, how they met.

'We met at Linnanmäki in the summer,' Minttu said.

'You've had a boyfriend for *months*?' I exclaimed unwillingly.

'Well, I…I…I was going to tell you one time but Niilo and Nea wouldn't leave us alone,' Minttu lied.

Did Niilo and Nea also steal your phone so you couldn't send me a message, I thought. She had got her first boyfriend, one of the most important events of her young life, and she hadn't even bothered to tell me. This was why she had stopped talking to me months ago. This was why she stopped wanting to see me.

Well, what did you expect, a part of me asked. She's a teenage girl with her first boyfriend. It is completely normal she wants her privacy and her independence. You are from her old life, from when she was a little girl. You're not part of her new life as a young woman and you just need to suck it up and deal with it. Every parent does it and you are nothing special. She doesn't need you anymore.

But what if I still need her?

Minttu was back to her running commentary about her life, but now I noticed a common thread in everything she said. This boy was the foundation of her existence. Minttu had fallen and scratched her arm the other day (while taking a walk with the boy). She had eaten the best hamburger last week (while with the boy). She had taken some selfies of her newly pink hair (to send to the boy). She had heard the funniest sexual innuendo (from the boy). Sometimes she couldn't stand just skating around the topic of him and blurted out random facts, like when his birthday was or how many siblings he had. She also explained why she didn't want to do anything with me the previous day: he came to see her (and had stayed the night).

I swallowed hard and didn't say anything. I just listened and remembered.

We parked in the car park at the Itis shopping mall and walked side-by-side to the doors. I couldn't stop glancing at her.

'Damn, you are tall,' I said. 'Almost as tall as me.'

She measured us with her eyes and stood experimentally on her toes.

'I'm as tall as you when I wear heels.'

'I remember that you like high heels. Do you want to get some today?'

'Maybe. I don't want any jeans because I hate the way they feel on my legs. I like jean shorts as long as they aren't too short. Here is okay.'

She indicated a point on her flank which was closer to her hipbone than her thigh. I started to smile at her joke but stopped when I saw she was serious. A teenage girl's definition of 'too short' was quite a bit different than mine, but I didn't want her to think of me as some out-of-touch old person.

'Summer is coming and it's time for Daisy Dukes,' I said. 'You can get anything you want while we are here, kul...Minttu.'

I needed to break my habit of calling her kulta, sweetie in Finnish. Minttu was too old for that now and I sounded patronising when I used it. Her terms of endearment should be coming from her boyfriend, not me.

'The first thing you need is new T-shirts,' I told her. 'What's up with this?'

I tugged her T-shirt. It had faded to a dull grey, the hems were ragged and there were a few small holes around her stomach. Her sweat pants didn't look much better and I suspected her coat was a hand-me-down from Mari.

'We don't have as much money as you,' Minttu snapped.

'Hey, don't be upset. I didn't mean anything by it.' I gave her a one-armed squeeze around her shoulders, which she accepted. 'You know, if you ever need any money all you have to do is ask.'

Minttu gave me a dismissive look and walked on.

We wandered up and down the mall, stopping and browsing in stores here and there. She picked out a couple of things she graciously let me buy for her, like T-shirts and sweatpants, but the only thing she specifically wanted was a face mask for acne. She chatted with the store clerk about the specific product she had wanted and seemed more excited about this than anything else we had purchased.

In a toy store she put a scarf on a stuffed dog's head and giggled. I giggled at her giggling, which made her giggle more. She was the cutest little girl ever, and I was hopelessly wrapped around her little finger. She accepted my homage with quiet dignity and never abused it. I forced her to pick the restaurant for lunch, and she chose an Italian place.

'Is this what you eat when you go to Sicily?' she asked.

'Not really,' I said. 'Most of these are kind of "International Italy" dishes which you can find anywhere. The food they serve in

Sicily is a lot different, except for the restaurants for tourists who expect this type of food.'

'Going to Sicily sounds so great. I've never flown to somewhere warm and stayed in a hotel. Are you going back for your birthday again?'

'That was the plan.'

She opened her mouth to say something more but a waitress appeared.

'Would you like a bottle of wine?' the waitress asked.

'No, thanks,' I said. 'Sparkling water for me, please.'

She turned to Minttu. 'Would you like a glass of wine? Maybe our house Chianti?'

'Still water, please,' Minttu said, her eyes wide.

When the waitress left to get our drinks we burst out laughing.

'I'm *fourteen*!' Minttu said.

'Was that the first time someone thought you were eighteen and old enough to drink?'

She nodded and I smiled.

'Well, you do act and look older than fourteen,' I said. 'You're a young woman now.'

'They're taking away women's rights in America.'

The sudden switch in topic caught me off guard. What made me even more flustered was how angry she looked. She stared accusingly at me, as if it was my fault and she was waiting for my defence she already knew would be inadequate. This was like when I first came to Finland and Finns considered me responsible for the Iraq War. The kindliest asked if I had left America because it was an oppressive regime trying to conquer the Middle-East. No, I had replied. I came here because of a woman. She was Heljä.

'Some people in America are trying to take away women's rights,' I admitted. 'But it's not all of America. Many people in many places want women's rights just like you have here. I feel bad to see what is happening there. I love my country but I don't feel at home there anymore.'

Minttu's attention had already shifted away from me; my disappointing justification was ignored without comment and she focused on the waitress giving us a basket of bread and olive oil. I was grateful to see her baffled. She had no idea what the little bowl of olive oil was for and the advantage shifted back to me. I explained how in Italy they tore off pieces of bread and dipped them in olive oil. It was much different from the bread spreads of Finnish cuisine, but after a tentative taste she pronounced it acceptable.

'I'm having fun today, Minttu,' I told her. 'I'm glad you let me take you shopping.'

'It's for you,' she said casually, letting excess oil drip from her bread before taking a bite.

I stared at the bread basket so I wouldn't meet her eye. For me. In my mind I was doing something for her. There was some vague patriarchal activity here, with the uncle picking up his niece, buying her things for her birthday and taking her home. She couldn't do these things herself; she needed help.

But she doesn't need *my* help, I knew. She had parents. Maybe they didn't have the disposable income which I had, but they were able to buy her anything she needed. Today's trip is not for her; it is for me. I had thought that I was the senior partner in this relationship but I was nothing of the sort.

Smart, sensitive Minttu had known that I had needed some companionship and had consented to it. She knew it had nothing to do with her birthday present. Most likely she only agreed to spend the day with me because she considered it an obligation, something she had to do because I wanted her to. Minttu was always responsible, doing what adults expected of her, yet sometimes this frustrated her, like the time with her mother's gloves. She would have preferred to watch her Netflix, mess around online or Snapchat with her boyfriend instead of being with me. I didn't want her to run to Kaarle for a hug and reassurance after being annoyed with me all day. I wanted her to run to me with her problems, like she had used to do. I wanted us to be friends, like we used to be.

'Do you remember the time I watched your old apartment when you guys were on holiday?' I asked her. 'You and Elias came back early and it was the first time we hung out together. We played Minecraft and walked to the store to get ice cream.'

'I remember,' she said.

'You rode your bike to your grandparents' house and I didn't want you to go alone. I was worried about you.'

'I did it every day!' Minttu laughed.

'It was a safe area and you knew what you were doing, but I was responsible for you.'

This didn't seem exactly right but I couldn't pin it down. I was trying to explain something to Minttu which I didn't understand myself. I still struggled with it, but Minttu had moved on and was telling me about the sauna ladle she made in handicrafts class. Yet she gave me a piercing look with those clear brown eyes as she talked.

Minttu's smart, I thought. She knows what I was trying to say and is leaving me to figure it out on my own.

After lunch we resumed our stroll, and she suddenly stopped to look in a store window. It was a lingerie store. Minttu calmly stood, nose up, shoulders back, hands on hips, as dispassionately interested as she had considered a hundred other displays. Mannequins in thongs. Mannequins in push-up bras. Mannequins in teddies. An hour ago I had been shopping with a little girl playing with a stuffed dog. Now I was shopping with a confident young woman, coolly considering lingerie without the slightest hint of self-consciousness or embarrassment.

My mind flashed back several years. It was the day I had abandoned Kaarle when Minttu demanded my attention. It was the day I had learned Minttu was reading my book. It was the day she had wanted stiletto heels for her school dance and I had smirked at

Kaarle's distress at her growing up.

I'm so sorry, Kaarle, I thought. I was so ignorant. I had no idea it could hurt this bad to see your child grow up. And she's not even my child. You've just loaned her to me.

'Do you want to go in?' I asked Minttu.

'Nah, I'm just looking,' she shrugged, turning back to me.

We walked away, me moving a bit faster than before to get away from that place. Maybe back to the toy store.

47

After we exhausted the stores in Itis I suggested we go to Kampen and wander around the stores there. Minttu reminded me to change the time card on the car—which I always forgot and which she always reminded me—and we took the metro downtown. Minttu was on the step above me on the escalator coming up from the metro platform, half turned towards me. The pendulum had swung. I wasn't going to dwell on how she had grown up and we had grown apart. Today had been a good day. A playful impulse struck me and I reached out and squeezed her knee.

'I'm not ticklish,' Minttu stated, looking at me without a smile.

'Yes, you are,' I said. 'And I know where you're ticklish.'

I poked her ribs, getting a squirm and laugh. I kept it up, trying to reach around her protecting arms as she laughed and twisted. This was an old custom with us. Back in the old days I would purposefully tickle her where she wasn't ticklish, she would scold me, and I would go for a different place. We always followed the same pattern. Sometimes I forgot where she was ticklish, and so did she. But it didn't matter. She always claimed to not be ticklish at my first attempt, and to laugh hysterically at my second, no matter where I tickled her. After a good hard tickle I relented and she leaned back against me affectionately.

My heart made a painful lurch. She had always hated public displays of affection. When she hugged me in front of others it was hesitantly, unwillingly, stoically, with that 'okay, I have to do this but I hope none of my friends see' mentality so pervasive in teenagers.

It was only when we were alone when she used to really grab me, squeezing me tight, like I was a piece of flotsam and she was a shipwreck survivor in the North Atlantic.

For the first time her affection for me overrode her public embarrassment and awkward self-consciousness.

Yes, we really were friends.

Suddenly my attention shot to a woman riding the down escalator opposite us. Bleached blond hair tied back to reveal long dark roots. Heavy and perfect make up. A newer but cheap spaghetti strap shirt under an open sweater. Her jaw was set; teeth clenched. She was studying the advertisements on her side of the tunnel to avoid looking at us. She had seen us and then carefully pretended she didn't. I stared at her for three long seconds as she slid past before I recognised her as Heljä, ex-wife, destroyer of worlds. She was right there, close enough to touch, close enough to spit on.

'Aren't you going to say hello to your niece, you fat cunt?' I said and did not say.

I cringed.

What kind of person was I, that an insult about her weight was the first thing I wanted to say to her? I had no idea what she was like now, but back when we were married her weight was what bothered her the most. I couldn't count how many diets, exercise machines, workout videos and nights spent weeping after a trip to the scale were tallied up during our marriage. I hate to admit it, but her weight had bothered me, too.

During our divorce I had told her *There is something wrong with your soul*, and I had firmly believed it. If you betray your spouse there is something fundamentally wrong with you.

But there was something wrong with my soul as well, in that I had eagerly reached out to poke her suppurating sore which wouldn't heal. It was an instinct of wickedness, jabbing the place which hurt her most.

But there was more. Here I was, sharing a fun moment with her niece. Minttu was my ex-wife's niece, not mine. I had no claim to her. What would I think if I had stumbled unexpectantly upon Heljä with a member of my family? Here I was with her niece as she watched from a distance, excluded. It must be devastating.

My ex-wife had betrayed my trust and faith and had cheated on me. She had broken the fundamental bond between partners who had committed to each other. Yet I had done something worse. I had stolen her family, or at least part of them. I had broken an even deeper familial bond, ripping away her brother's family and claiming them for my own.

I was the evil one, not her.

Why did I stay in Finland, now that I had the skills and resources to live anywhere in the world? I could have gone somewhere with more sun and less taxes, but I stayed here. I still didn't know why I was here. Why had I integrated myself with my ex-wife's brother and his family in the first place? Did I do this because I genuinely liked them, or did I do this to hurt Heljä?

I tried to tell myself that of course I genuinely liked them, but a quiet and persistent voice continued. Then why did I try to fuck Heljä's friend right after the divorce? Why did I always post in Swedish on her aunt's Facebook page, if not to shove it in her face: I am speaking the language you hate with your aunt. Why did I always ask Kaarle if Heljä was coming to their family events, if not to make sure they wouldn't invite her? Why was my first reaction to taunt Heljä about her niece being with me, and not her?

I looked at Minttu with dawning horror. She wasn't my special niece at all. She and her family were my secret weapon against that woman who had caused me such pain.

Yet Minttu was telling me about making meatballs at her home economics class at school. Both of us liked to cook. It was something we shared. She had turned around, going backwards up the escalator, facing me as she told me about ingredients and the big stove in their classroom and how classmate so-and-so couldn't make meatballs and everyone had laughed at the malformed balls, including their creator.

She was completely focused upon me and ignored the world around her. I reached out, gently touched her arm and drew her attention to the approaching landing coming up behind her.

We were almost at the end of our ride.

Book III—My Land

1

WHEN WE RETURNED to Kaarle and Mari's Minttu was still chatting away like normal but I knew something had changed, irretrievably broken. All the king's horses and all the king's men couldn't put Humpty back together again.

Minttu took her things into her room and I went into the living room where Kaarle was playing a game on the computer.

'What happened with Nea?' he asked. 'You know how sensitive she is and how self-conscious she is about her English.'

'I don't know. No: yes, I do. I'm sick. There's something wrong with me. I can't eat. I can't sleep. I can't write, and I'm a writer.' Suddenly the words were pouring out of me. I couldn't stop them if I had tried.

'I'm tired,' I told him. 'I don't mean physically or emotionally. I'm existentially tired. I'm just tired of everything. I'm tired of trying and failing to be part of this country. I'm angry at myself for not being capable of being Finnish. I hate myself for not being able to learn the Finnish language and took it out on Nea because she is no good with English. Why the fuck am I in Finland? There is no point.'

Kaarle leaned back in his chair and looked at me, silent.

'We saw Heljä. On the escalator in Kampen. It was the first time I saw her since I moved out. The reason I always come to your family events is so you don't invite her. I've been using all of you to hurt her.'

My words echoed in the room like the sound of a guillotine blade.

'I don't believe that,' Kaarle said.

'It's true,' I said. 'I need to stay away from you and your family.'

'You're part of our family,' he said.

'No, I'm not. I never was and I never will be. I can never be Finnish and I can never be part of your family. It's time to quit pretending. Now I need to go back and say goodbye to your daughters.'

Minttu was messaging her boyfriend and Nea was playing a game on her computer. Nea brightened up when she saw me.

'I sent you a message!' she said. 'Our birthday party is in two weeks.'

'I won't be here.'

Minttu looked up.

'Why not?' Nea cried.

I shrugged. 'Maybe you should invite your real family, not me.'

Nea considered this a moment and threw herself backwards, hugging herself, weeping. I stared at her, waiting for that instinct to kick in, like it had so many times before, when I would run to her at the first instant of real or fake distress. But I felt nothing. I simply stood and watched her cry.

'I'm sorry for everything. Seriously. I really am.'

I turned to leave but Nea caught hold of my hand.

'You promised we would go to the action park!'

'It's better if we didn't go.'

'Today you took *Minttu*!'

'Okay, okay,' I sighed. 'We'll go.'

I had no intention of taking her. I just said that to shut her up. Nea's snuffles quieted and a hesitant smile appeared. She didn't understand what I was doing, but Minttu did. Minttu stared straight into my eyes for one second, two seconds, three seconds… until her phone beeped and she immediately dismissed me. She looked at her phone and her thumbs flicked away as she talked to her boyfriend. She was utterly indifferent to whether I was part of her life or not. This was worse than hate, and I thanked her for it. This would make it easier.

2

'Varje år dör hundratals personer som inte har några arvingar,' I read on Yle's news site. 'Om man efter släktutredning konstaterar att det inte finns några laga arvingar och den avlidna inte heller lämnat ett testamente efter sig, tillfaller kvarlåtenskapen staten.'

I turned my head and looked out of the window, to the dead heather in flower boxes hanging from my balcony railing, the bare trees in the courtyard dripping water from their bony branches and the wet grey building opposite, with its blank windows reflecting the eternally grey sky. Piles of black snow, stained with mud and the tiny stones which were spread on roads and sidewalks. I sat and looked a long time, ignoring the periodic chirps from my computer insisting that I immediately read the emails from clients coming in.

Fuck Finland.

Turning away from the world I picked up my phone and scrolled through my contact list until I found a name and called him.

'Hej Tuomas,' I said. 'I know you are a corporate lawyer, but could you recommend a personal attorney to help me make a will? It's simple: no complicated assets or relationships. No family in Finland.'

'Yes, I could recommend someone, but if it is simple I could do it.'

There followed a series of emails with me explaining what I wanted and Tuomas' assistant sending draft versions of my Last Will and Testament. It was short and sweet, just a few paragraphs long.

'Do you want to put in any instructions for memorial services?' the assistant asked. 'Or disposition of remains?'

'I don't give a shit,' I wrote back. 'That's for the people left behind and they don't care either.'

'Then the last thing we need is personal identity codes of the people named in the will.'

'Is that necessary?'

'It isn't strictly required, but it is a good idea. A testament is to reflect the will of the decadent how his assets will be disbursed, so you want to be as clear as possible so there are no misunderstandings.'

At my next Swedish lesson with Tapio we spoke briefly about our mutual friend, Fran Weaver, who had died from cancer. Fran had edited all the books which I wrote and Tapio published. All three of us had a custom of gathering several times a year, either in a bar downtown or out at Tapio's place for a sauna. The talk of his death gave me an easy segue.

'Ursäkta mig, men jag ska prata engelska nu,' I told Tapio. 'I'm making a will. I'm naming you as my literary executor and I need your personal identity code.'

Tapio was surprised. 'What does that entail?'

'You're in charge of all the business affairs relating to my writing. You change the copyrights with the publishers so the royalties go to the right person. You can also dig through all my unpublished stuff to see if any of it is salvageable, which it probably isn't.'

He looked at me and thought for a moment.

'It sounds interesting and I'll do it,' he said, and suddenly realised he sounded too eager. 'But I hope it doesn't happen for a long time.'

My next call was to Kaarle.

'Once upon a time I saw that Minttu was reading one of my books,' I told him. 'I was surprised that she was interested in it, but then I realised that she didn't care about the book. She cared about me.'

'Of course she does. All the kids do.'

'Well, I cared about them, too, because they were the closest things to a family I had in this country. I'm making my will. I'm naming Minttu as my literary heir so I need her personal identity code.'

'Holy shit,' Kaarle said.

'Everything else is being split equally between her, Nea and Niilo, so I need their codes too. It's just my way of saying sorry.'

'I don't know what to say.'

'Say their personal identity codes.'

'I don't have them memorised, but I can text their codes to you.'

'Tack. I don't know if you need it or not, but I'll send you a copy of the will.'

'I hope it doesn't happen for a long time.'

'Why does everyone keep saying that? Who the fuck cares?'

3

'If someone wants to go out into the wilderness and camp undisturbed where could he go?' I messaged Robert.

'How about an island?' he messaged back. 'Isoholma in Teijo national park.'

'Perfect.'

'There won't be anyone there this time of year.'

'That's exactly what I want.'

'Do you have appropriate gear? It will be very cold and very wet.'

'I have everything.'

'Tell me.'

Robert was doubtful, for good reason. It was early spring in southern Finland. It was that cocktease time of year, when you think pleasant weather is just around the corner only to be disappointed week after week after week. The mercury kept dipping below zero and bouncing back above. Rain, sleet, snow. Grey mud, grey sky, grey world, grey soul. I had to give him a list of everything I intended on taking with me, including their price to give an indication of their quality, before he was satisfied. Tent, sleeping bag, clothes, food, hatchet, rain coat, gloves, boots…

'Don't worry,' I messaged him. 'I camped all the time in the winter in America.'

'This isn't Indiana,' he replied.

I took a train to the west. The sad buildings of Helsingfors gave way to the sad trees of Esbo and beyond. He picked me up at the train station and we drove south. We followed narrow winding roads to the coast and a small boat ramp. He backed his trailer into the sea and I sat in the boat so it didn't float away while he parked his car. Soon we were going south into the face of a bitter wind as the shore fell away from both sides. In front of us was a lonely forested island with grey cliffs.

'It's easy to get there but it might not be so easy to get off. The island is in the middle of an estuary with a big river flowing into it. If ice upriver breaks free this will be impassable.'

'Menföre,' I yelled over the engine and wind. 'That's fine by me.'

I sat in the bow and could feel him looking at me. I turned around to face him, Robert, my friend, my psychopomp. 'Is everything okay?' he asked.

'Nothing is okay,' I said, and turned my face back to the island.

The bottom of the boat grated on a gravel shore. A few ancient and faded plastic bottles lay on the beach, deposited by the melting ice. We climbed a steep hillside, lugging up my gear.

'I brought a bag of dry wood,' Robert said. 'You'll need it

because all the wood will be wet. Use it sparingly, because that's all you will have. Keep it dry.'

I nodded. On top of the hill was one of those little wooden lean-tos and metal firepits which are scattered around public land in Finland. There were names written on the walls, scratched with burnt sticks. Jussi. Per-Erik. Mika. Juhannus 2016. I surveyed them like they were prehistoric cave paintings. It began to spit cold rain.

'If you see any mushrooms or fungi, don't touch them,' Robert said. 'Nothing good grows this time of year. I'm serious.'

I didn't nod this time.

'Three days is a long time to be out in this weather. I've taught you what I know about Finland's nature, but you still don't respect it. You're on your own.'

I nodded again.

Robert hurried away, like he didn't want to be there. That was understandable. It was a dreary world. Standing on the hilltop, I waited until he was out of sight. I turned my back on the ocean and walked into the forest.

The trees were emaciated sticks. Pines with dead branches, naked birches, unidentifiable anorexic trees. Scraggly bushes like a slow-moving cancer. There was mud. So much mud. I searched for and found a place on higher ground with a flat-ish, bare-ish area to pitch my tent. I put it up in the dead wet grass next to a fallen spruce. I stashed my backpack inside and went back to the lean-to, where I sat alone in the bark dust of summers past and stared through the falling rain.

4

'Were his eyes open?' my sister Ann wanted to know.

'No,' I said. 'They were closed.'

'Did he shoot himself?' my brother Wayne asked.

'No,' I said. 'He did not.'

I had been home from college for a short winter break when Dad died. In the morning Mom found him on the bathroom floor and woke me. Dad was taken away before Wayne and Ann could arrive. Each of my siblings wanted to question me alone. They wanted clues to how he had passed from life to death, his last thought, his last emotion.

Wayne's question expressed a deep fear which we had shared. As Dad got progressively worse I had wondered how much he could take, how far he could go. The constant torturous pain ineffectually treated with massive amounts of opioids. Would it eventually get so bad that Dad would break and say no, I can't take any more.

He did not. Dad never broke. He was Catholic. He prayed in Latin. He had a personal relationship with his God and believed that suicide was a mortal sin.

5

I sat cross-legged, hugging myself against the cold, as I thought. Pulling off the glove on my right hand, I dug deep into a pocket for my phone to check my social media accounts. I couldn't find what I was looking for inside myself so hoped I could find it there. Cindy, my friend from America, had posted pictures from her birthday party. She was surrounded by her husband, sisters and kids. I looked at it for a long time. It was so different from how I spent my birthdays, alone with a glass of wine in some Sicilian village, trying to tell myself that 'Happy Birthday!' messages on Facebook were just as good as people actually wanting to be with me.

Years from now, when this solid matriarch was on her deathbed, Cindy would still be surrounded by all these people. Her kids and grandkids and maybe great-grandkids. Who would be with me at the end? I would have my bitter memories and my books which no one reads. Which one of us would be happier with their life?

This was the choice I made. So be it.

There was a pine tree off to my right with a faded white circle spraypainted on it about head high. Farther away I saw another tree with another circle. Some semblance of a hiking path, marked a number of years ago. I got up, pulled the hood over my head, and followed it through the cold Finnish forest.

6

Twenty years after Dad died someone found an old recording of him. My sister emailed it to me. I knew his voice, but it was also a stranger's voice. I was surprised by the Southern twang to it, which I did not remember. It had been so long.

When a person dies the body lingers for a time before returning to the earth from which it came. The process can be delayed for a time through embalming and sealed caskets, but it can only be delayed, not stopped. The same is true for memory. You can try to preserve the memory through books or memorial wings at hospitals or giant pyramids, but these are simply a rearguard action against the inevitable obliteration.

Probably some of my family and friends will mourn me, at least a little bit, and at least for a time. But I'm already dead to many of them. I go back to America and see my friends' babies are now teenagers, they have swapped one spouse for another, they have new houses and jobs, there is more grey in their hair. I have missed so much. I go back to America and look around in amazement at all the changes, like a ghost of someone who died in 2005 and still wanders the earth. The present has no place for the dead.

Others won't remember me at all. I have so many acquaintances in Finland. We have the type of relationship where you say 'oh, how terrible' if you hear they have died. You might go to their funeral if you aren't busy. That sort of relationship.

I look at Nea and wonder what she will think when I die. She seems to adore me, but she is young, and the young are resilient. She would be disconsolate for an hour and sad for a day and then move on. In five years she would struggle to remember my name.

Maybe a brief whisper of me will continue for another

generation or so. Somebody might be cleaning out an old house and find a yellowed book with my name on it. They might open it up randomly, curious as to whether it should be saved or not, and then toss it out. Perhaps when Minttu is old and grey she will tell her grandkids that she honed her English by playing with an American uncle who loved to spoil her. These grandkids might remember that story for a time, or they might not. But in a short period of time all memory of me will be gone.

It bothers me. I want to be remembered. I want to have had a positive impact on the people around me. But I wish I didn't want these things. I know they are illusory, a phantom, something I can't control and shouldn't want to control.

Yet there is something deep in humanity that longs for a continuance. Many people need to have hope of an afterlife. Our evolution has programmed us to survive and reproduce, and everything beyond that is an appendix to your life. I don't have hope in an afterlife and doubt I will ever have kids, so the two hopes of humanity are lost to me.

I wish to leave my body out in the woods. I'd be fine with that. Let a hunter stumble upon my gnawed bones a couple moose seasons after I died. Let him see the dirt between my teeth. I've been a failure at life so let my nutrients be useful in death. Let me be forgotten as quickly as possible. Just get it over with.

I'm not Dad. I can't take it anymore.

7

There was no wind, no songs of birds, no boats. I stopped walking and listened, but the only sounds were those on the verge of consciousness: rare drops of water, a branch squeaking against a tree, tired waves from the distant shore. It was just me and Finland.

The path was not easy to follow. It had not been walked upon since the previous autumn. Branches and leaves obscured it and the melting snow had blurred its edges. The white circles on the trees were faded and not always easily seen. Sometimes a tree which had been painted had fallen. Yet the route made sense. When I couldn't find the next marked tree I simply chose the way which seemed best, and soon another white dot appeared. I followed the path unconsciously, and thought.

8

'Why did you come to Finland?' is what everyone always asks, and my answer has always been: 'Because I married a Finn.'

That's a lie. I've been lying about this for fourteen years.

If Heljä had been my next-door neighbour in Indianapolis I would never have been interested in her. Not as a spouse. Not as a lover. Not even as a friend. The only thing that attracted me to her was that she lived in Finland and wanted me to join her. I was more optimistic and excited about the opportunity to live in Finland than to get married, even though I never said it or even thought it, at least consciously.

The truth is that I came to Finland because I wanted a change. All my friends were getting married and having kids and settling down in their Midwestern homes, but I was looking at the far horizons of the soul and wondering if they could be reached by passing the far horizons of the world. I couldn't stay at home because I was an outsider. Maybe somewhere out there I would find what I was looking for.

Looking back at those years of courtship and first years of marriage many wonderful memories come to mind: seeing the Orthodox cathedral in Helsinki, feeding cherries to the gulls at the harbour, going to a summer cabin on the shores of Pyhäjärvi in Säkylä, seeing Yö in concert, getting drunk at student parties… But none of these memories were about my wife. She was only my native fixer. All of those memories were about experiencing Finland, finally looking over that horizon at what the world and life is like outside of the cornfields of Indiana. I didn't come to Finland because I married a Finn. I married a Finn because I wanted to come to Finland in the hopes that I would finally cease being an outsider. I used her. It's no wonder she did what she did, after the evil I had done to her.

I stumbled to a halt on my hike and threw the hood of my coat back so I could see clearly. It was like coming to after a blackout and seeing a dead body on the floor in front of me and a smoking gun in my hand.

I don't know what happened, I called the world to witness. I don't remember anything.

Yes, I do. Look deeper.

It was raining at our wedding so we hired a big tent. It was dim and dreary with battered hired tables and chairs laid out like a wake. Old men huddled in the corner of a makeshift stage, holding their instruments and looking at their ancient watches. Someone said it was time so everyone stood, and I took my place at the head of the tent to wait for her. Heljä appeared in the doorway wearing her wedding dress and on her father's arm. She raised a foot to begin walking to me and time stopped. A window opened. At that moment I looked through and saw the truth. I knew exactly what I was doing. The gift of foresight was given me for a brief instant, and I knew it was all wrong. It would start badly, continue badly and end badly. Because of me, who I was and what I had done.

Goddamn, Heljä, I thought. I'm so sorry, but an apology will never make up for this.

9

My path ended at an obstruction. High winds at some point in the recent past had knocked down a wide swath of trees. I looked to the left, where the deadfall was worst, and to the right, where the ground fell away in a cliff. I fell to my knees in the wet moss and pine needles and reindeer grass and leprotic blueberry bushes. There, directly in front of me, under the first tree of the deadfall, was a deathcap mushroom.

It could not be a deathcap. It was only March, months before mushrooms would make their first appearance.

Wait. Was it March? I looked around myself at the bare trees, the falling rain, the mud, the dead moss, the gaunt bushes, the grey, always the grey. Far off I heard the call of an elk. The sound glided through the trees effortlessly. This could be any month. This was Finland Eternal. Maybe I had come unstuck in time.

I got down on my stomach and wriggled under the dead tree until the mushroom was three centimetres from my face. The dripping water splashed coldly on my head and speckled my glasses. The mushroom had the white stipe supporting the gilled cap. Always avoid religion and women, Robert had said: any mushroom with a steeple or a skirt.

Backing out from under the tree I got back on my feet and studied the deadfall. The island had narrowed considerably and I was close to the tip. Going over the deadfall was impossible. It stretched from the cliff on my right to the water on my left, a twisted, tormented pile of tortured trees.

I took off my gloves and coat. I removed my sweatshirt, woollen shirt and T-shirt. Off came the boots, socks, jeans, long underwear and underwear. Back on my knees, I plucked the mushroom and looked at the bulbous root for a moment before I stuck it in my mouth, chewed and swallowed. Dirt between my teeth.

I walked down the hill towards my left, my bare feet pierced by sodden branches and brown pine needles at every step. The shoreline was marshy and the mud was deep. I had to go out quite a way before I couldn't feel the bottom. I pushed all the air out of my lungs, dunked my head underwater and took a huge breath of cold, muddy water.

10

Everyone always asks why I came to Finland. No one asks why I am still here. I'm here because I love Finland. I love the rule of law and individual freedoms and collective responsibilities. I love the education and the health system and the taste of blueberries in July. I love the smell of wood smoke in a sauna and *The Unknown Soldier*. I love the xenophobes and the social awkwardness and the alcoholics and the mud and rain and yes, even the eternal clouds. I hate them and love them as I hate and love myself.

I love the people. I love Robert for being my mentor and for introducing me to the land, the trees, the water, the mushrooms. I love Kaarle and Mari for adopting me into their family. I love their kids so much that I give them everything. Split my shit, Niilo, Nea and Minttu. And Minttu, you're my literary heir. Everything I have ever written is yours. I'm sorry it is worthless, but it was the best I could do.

Too bad I had fucked it all up. Too bad I had hurt so many people. Too bad that Heljä was right all along. I wanted to be a martyr but instead I was a murderer. Suicide is a mortal sin, and I am not as strong as Dad.

11

The water shot me out and my entire torso contracted. A huge gush of brackish water and solids burst out of my mouth. I gasped a few times and more came out.

My feet skidded on submerged, mud-covered rocks. The shoreline waited in front of me. Unsteadily, I walked ashore. Mud caked my feet and I was dripping water, but I did not shiver. I wasn't cold at all. The deadfall was to my right so I had passed it while in the water. I climbed back up the hill and stood upon the path. It went down the backbone of the island to the southern tip, where I could see a brightening, an openness between the trees. I was almost there.

It was easy to walk up the path now on the gentle slope. There at the tip of the island was another fire pit and outhouse for campers. Naked, I walked onto the huge bare bedrock jutting out from the end of the island ten metres above the sea and looked out. The estuary opened out there, arms wide to embrace the Baltic, and the sun suddenly broke through the clouds and shone on me.

Nea, I thought. I need the Finnish Maiden. She is the key to everything.

12

Mari's mother and father were watching Niilo while Kaarle and Mari ran errands. Minttu was also gone, away at her boyfriend's.

I was glad they weren't there. I wanted to tell them how important they were to me, but I had no idea how to do it. I was going to learn on Nea. I was somehow going to explain the depth and complexity of my feelings to someone with only a few hundred words' vocabulary in English. She was the key. She was Finland.

After short hellos and goodbyes to Niilo and his grandparents Nea and I went outside. She took my hand and, instead of going to the car, walked me into the yard to face the tall pine trees.

'What's going on?' I asked her.

'Listen,' she said.

My arm went around her shoulder and hers went around my waist, and we stood to face the Finnish forest. Almost immediately I knew what she had been trying to show me.

'You wanted me to hear that, didn't you?' I asked her. 'Snow falling on pine trees is the voice of God.'

Snow fell down, ever so gently, in the breezeless air. You could hear it touch the pine needles all around us. The sound was on the verge of hearing and yet all pervasive, everywhere. Nea looked up with a smile on her face. She bared her throat to me, perfectly trusting. Snowflakes landed on her nose to turn into drops of water or on her eyelashes to survive, entrapped, for a few moments longer.

I stepped away from her and Nea raised an arm to the falling snow. She spun, laughing, and her long coat flared out around her knees. For once instant Nea looked exactly like the shape of Finland on the map. There she is, I thought. There is the Finnish Maiden.

13

'Stay close to me,' I told Nea. 'I want to be able to see you.'

'Okay,' she said, and for a while she listened to me.

We were at the adventure park. It was Saturday so the place was packed with kids. Nea was a barely-suppressed chaos of excitement, flying from one activity to another. The trampoline, the climbing wall, the basketball court, the tumbling mat.

In frequent bursts of affection Nea ran to me and snapped a vice-like hug around my neck, her face pressed against my chest. This wouldn't go on much longer. She was on the cusp of teenhood. Already I had noticed groups of young boys elbowing each other and drawing attention to her. Check out the blond, they were saying. Nea ignored them with dignified aloofness, but she knew she was being admired. Soon Nea would be like Minttu, more interested in boys than having anything to do with me.

At first, she stopped in her headlong flight, waiting for me to catch up and remembering that I wanted to keep her in sight. Yet going from one activity to the next was like a hazardous journey through dangerous territory. Nea ran ahead and disappeared behind crowds of people. I had to push through, not politely, to keep close.

The burden of responsibility began to shift towards me. It was no longer her job to stay close to me: it was my job to stay close to her. She ducked and twisted through the crowds, and I hurried to stay up with her.

'Don't go so fast,' I told her. 'I want to stay close to you.'

'Okay,' she said, either not understanding or choosing not to.

Anxiety slowly built. Finland is a safe place, compared to most of the Western world, but things do happen here. This little girl was under my responsibility. Her parents allowed me to take her, trusting me even after I had inexcusably hurt her. This was not like forgetting to water a friend's houseplants while she was on holiday. This was someone's baby girl.

Anxiety started to shift to anger. Not only towards Nea, but towards the people who continually wandered in front of me, cutting that lifeline of visual sight between us. I shoved through families of swarming parents and kids, trying to follow her skinny form as it darted through crowds of people.

I shouldered my way through one large group, knocking people out of the way, and came into a human clearing. Nea was gone. I looked right and left. There were dozens of little blond girls running back and forth, but no Nea. The Finnish Maiden was gone.

I became frantic, spinning in a circle trying to find her. Guessing that she went back towards her favourite trampoline, I shoved through the wall of people and emerged into another clearing, a glade of calmness in the centre of humanity.

A vision came. The man I had always worried about was here. He had finally struck. A tall, faceless man had a grip on Nea's wrist and was leading her away. She was resisting, but not frantic. Nea was looking back over her shoulder, looking for me, with a dawning horror on her face.

I stepped out of myself; terror replaced anxiousness; fury replaced terror. In my vision I came at the man. Words, rationality, coherent thought were gone, replaced by flashes of emotions and images. I had the man on the ground and went for his throat, not with hands but with my teeth.

Bridges and crowns cracked and gave way in my mouth, never designed for this. I tore the thick, rubbery skin away and snapped the jugular with a wet pop. The shrieks of the onlookers were drowned out by the sound of spilling blood. I clamped on the windpipe, feeling it collapse between my jaws. I could feel air whishing through a corner of the windpipe still open, so I changed my grip and gnawed it closed.

I was staggered, struggling to stay upright as the vision possessed me. All traces of the modern world were gone, and I was living a million years ago, when a hominid ancestor had a rival tribe member on the ground by the throat when his young were threatened.

Vaguely my sight returned, and I was stumbling on the unnaturally bright concrete amidst crowds of people. It was the unalterable truth, superseding the laws of God, man or physics: if someone were to hurt this little girl I would taste the last feeble spurts of their heart's blood.

I had been wrong. I hadn't made friends with Kaarle and his family to hurt my ex-wife. I wasn't worried about my responsibility as an adult watching Nea. I was worried about *her.* That was the case with Minttu riding her bike alone to her grandparents that long-gone summer day. I cared for *them.*

The faceless man, the vision I had repeatedly of someone hurting the girls, was me. You can never see your own face. In a mirror, yes; in a picture, yes; but not with your own eyes. Not the way other people see you. I had always been afraid that I would hurt the kids, just like I had hurt Heljä.

I was baffled the whole world continued on as before, and not everyone and everything was flattened, spreading out in concentric circles from me, ground zero to this reality.

But the massive psychic shock reached one person.

The crowd of people parted and I saw a blond girl. Nea was running away from me, heading towards the trampoline, when the force of my devotion hit her. She skidded to a stop and tore back towards me, hair flying behind her in the wind, knees wobbly in that ubiquitous little girl way, her face shining with joy brighter than the sun.

The Finnish Maiden slammed into me and wrapped her arms around my neck, her gaze turned up to mine.

I grabbed her head, intertwining my fingers in her long blond hair, and bent my face into her sun, our noses almost touching. This was it, I realised with perfect clarity. She was almost a teen and Nea would never run to me like this again.

'I love you, too,' I finally said.

14

I was delayed at Catania airport by a diligent carabiniere who thought I looked like a marijuana enthusiast and a non-diligent airline who lost my luggage. My driver had waited, thankfully, but he was in a hurry. I wanted to stop and admire restless Mount Etna spewing ash and steam, but my driver didn't even look at it. He saw it every day, so he no longer saw it. By the time I got to my hotel on the island of Ortygia in Syracuse it was late and I was tired. The hotel restaurant was closed—March wasn't tourist season—so I was left hungry.

'We offer free international phone calls, even back to America,' the front desk clerk said, looking at my US passport.

'I'm Finnish,' I told him. 'I have an American passport, but my land is Finland.'

'You can call Finland, too,' he said. 'I have always wanted to visit. What is it like?

'Cold and rainy and cloudy.'

'Everything is white?'

'Everything is grey. Sicily is defined by its sun, but Finland is defined by its clouds and greyness. Sicily's climate is physically brutal, but Finland's is mentally and spiritually brutal.'

'That is too bad.'

'No, it is beautiful. It is a wonderful place and I love it. Sisu, the concept of stoic perseverance, could never have developed here. The Baltic is even more beautiful than the Mediterranean.'

He looked doubtful but smiled, because the customer is always right.

'You should come back in the summer when you can swim in the sea,' he said.

'I will swim in the sea now. The cold does not bother me.'

My room was decadent and luxurious. I had chosen one of the best rooms in one of the best hotels in the city. It had been an ancient manor house from the 1700s which had been in ruins for decades before recently being restored into a hotel. The furnishings gave a sense of that era, like a misty photograph, with flagstone floors, a giant four poster bed, a shower larger than my entire bathroom back in Helsinki. I sat down at the elegant little escritoire and opened my phone.

The day before I had flown out of Helsinki I had sent an email to Tapio.

'Do you remember how I told you that someday I would send ten pages of something I wanted you to read?' I had written. 'Here it is.'

The first line was: 'I chose one of those apartments where they find a months-old suicide after neighbours complain about an odd smell.'

Within an hour Tapio had emailed me back: 'Send me the first thirty pages.'

I had done so from the airport and now I read his response:

'This is good. I am surprised,' he said, 'But you must be careful about characterisation. For example, I liked how you are scared of your brother.'

Well, that makes one of us, I thought. I love Wayne and I don't want to be scared of him.

Switching to Facebook I saw a post from Mari. With help from Google Translate I puzzled out that Minttu wanted to take guitar in music class at school. Did anyone have a guitar she could use, or an old one they could buy?

I scrolled down the messaging app, trying to find Minttu. She was far down the list.

'I hear you are looking for a guitar,' I messaged her. 'Did I ever tell you I played the guitar in college?'

'No. I didn't know that.'

'If you want, I'll help you pick one out when I get back from Sicily.'

'I heard that you're in Sicily again.'

'Yes. I'm here for my birthday. Your birthday is in three days and mine is in four days. But do you want the guitar?'

'Yes of course thank you so much.'

'I'm happy to do it. You're my niece and I love you.'

'I love you too,' she said. 'I was talking about you and one of my friends said that if I ever asked you would take me to Sicily with you.'

'Of course I would,' I wrote. 'It would be fun to have you here,' I wrote, and then finally but inevitably the hint Minttu was dropping landed on my head. 'Do you want to come to Sicily so we can celebrate our birthdays together?' I asked.

'Yes I do,' she answered.

'Do you seriously want to take a ten-day holiday with me? You'll miss your boyfriend while you're gone.'

'I miss my uncle now.'

I stared at the words until they blurred in my vision. Minttu hadn't been indifferent to me being in her life or not. I had mistaken her pain for indifference. I had hurt her and she had raised her defences to protect herself, just like she always did. But now for the first time she was not afraid to show vulnerability and say she needed me just like I needed her. My fingers were wet with tears as I tried to type a reply.

'Will you ask your parents if you can come?'

'I will ask. I think they will say yes.'

'I think they will say yes too.'

15

Kaarle and Mari were co-consuls. Nothing happened in their household without unanimous approval. I couldn't speak with Mari, but she had always supervised my relationships with her children. From the very beginning, the first time I played with the kids when I housesat for them, Mari's smile or frown determined what would happen or would not happen. If she had said one word when she saw me dangling Nea upside down—ei—then none of those relationships would have happened.

She and Kaarle said yes. They didn't only say yes about me

buying their daughter an expensive birthday holiday, or about her spending several days with me. They said yes to me being their kids' uncle, with all the rights and responsibilities that entails. They thought a relationship with me was good for their kids, and maybe they thought it was good for me, too. No longer would I struggle to define my relationships with them. Niilo is my godson and nephew. Nea and Minttu are my nieces. End of story.

Everyone asks why I came to Finland but no one asks why I am still here. If anyone ever does, now I have an answer: I'm still in Finland because some Finns adopted me. I'll always be an outsider, but that doesn't mean I can't be happy and have healthy relationships.

16

I woke up the next morning at 6:03. Out on the balcony I watched the sun rise over the Mediterranean. The Mediterranean is so different from the Baltic, which is so different from the Ohio River. I got dressed and went out, leaving my phone behind. I crossed a tiny road, carefully checking for cars. In Finland the drivers are responsible for not hitting pedestrians. In Sicily pedestrians are responsible for not getting hit.

This city of Syracuse was where St. Lucy, the bringer of light, lived and died. Here is her tomb and her likeness in silver, but her spirit flies to the far North when we need her most, when the women wear crowns of burning tapers during the darkest time of the year.

I walked south along the edge of the island, on a sidewalk about five metres above the water, stopping occasionally to watch the little fishing boats out on Homer's wine dark sea. I passed old churches, half-ruinous buildings erected out of yellow stone when America was a British colony and Finland was part of Sweden. One, the Chiesa dello Spirito Santo, drew me to it. It had a dome at one end and a towering façade on the other, with empty niches for statues of long-dead saints and tiny flowers and blades of grass growing between the stones. My left hand touched the warm stone and my right hand touched my forehead, my heart, my left shoulder, my right shoulder. Maybe God had spoken to me with that long-ago coin flip.

At the end of the island and the old fortress I turned north along the western edge. It was about twenty degrees, good enough for a T-shirt for someone used to Finnish weather. It would be even warmer late in the afternoon when I picked up Minttu at the airport. As I walked I came across a few locals, men like me mostly, who rose with the sun and were just coming out. It wasn't tourist season so I was the only non-native on the streets. I looked like a pasty-faced Finn but at least I was smart enough not to wear socks and sandals.

I looked out over the Grand Harbour, where the Romans sailed in their wrath and Archimedes used his ingenuity to defend his city. Technology had failed in the face of determination, and Syracuse fell. Archimedes was killed in the sack and Marcellus, five times consul, took Syracuse and made Sicily Roman. I walked on.

Just beyond I came to the Spring of Arethusa. Arethusa is a water nymph from the Peloponnese who had fled the unwanted advances of the river god Alpheus. She passed under the Mediterranean to spill out her fresh water there at the edge of the island. She failed, though, as do most émigrés. Alpheus simply followed her and mixed his waters with hers.

When the Greek colonists arrived 2,750 years ago they said that the water was from their land in Greece, gushing forth there in their new home. Arethusa was so important to them they put her head on their coins, surrounded by dolphins. Expats always long for the homes of their birth.

I stood on the edge and looked at her, with her papyrus and ducks and fish. She came from underground out into a large half-circular stone structure, but she wasn't contained by it. Her fresh water passed through a small channel to rush out into the Mediterranean like she has done for thousands of years.

I went up to a little café above the spring, the only place open so early. A few locals were there, chatting before going to work. I was visibly a foreigner and everyone looked closely at me.

'Prego,' the waiter said-asked.

'Un espresso. Dubbel—mi scusi—doppio.'

He gave me my coffee and I dug into my pocket for coins.

'What are you doing?' he asked.

'I'm paying for my coffee.'

'No you are not. This is not tourist season so don't act like a tourist. Act like a Sicilian. Sit down and enjoy your coffee. Watch the fishing boats and the sun on the harbour. Only after you have done these things will you pay.'

I sat down on a stool at a little table and sipped the espresso. It was marvellous. It tasted of rich Sicilian earth, of pasta and citrus and men grasping hands and kissing each other on the cheek, unashamed because they loved each other. American and Finnish coffee didn't taste like this. Coffee is always better in the next place.

Far out on the Mediterranean was a little red wooden fishing boat. All the other boats had two or sometimes more people in them, but this boat only had one. As I watched the lone fisherman pulled in a catch. He held it sparkling in the morning light for a moment, letting the world admire it even though there was no one with him to see, before putting it in the bottom of his boat.

Grave old men arrived in immaculate outdated suits with ugly young men in sunglasses behind them. Everyone falls silent and stand aside. Who were they? Cosa Nostra, Bottaro-Attanasio? Or just respected old locals being driven by their pious grandsons? The old men deign to notice me. They stare at me for a long moment. They look at me and I look at them. The Sicilians are not like the Finns. They use fierce eye contact with anyone they see. I am an unknown, where I shouldn't be. I nod, slowly and respectfully. I will kiss their rings, if they allow it. I want to feel the metal under my lips. I have always wanted to belong. They nod back and the young men in sunglasses look away.

The old men drink coffee and talk softly to men who emerged from deep in the café, gesticulating in that manual language I want to learn. When they have concluded their business the old men walk away to their cars, and everyone waits until they are gone before the morning conversation resumes. I am still there, in the centre of it all, tasting my sublime coffee.

When I am finished I pay and make a request from the surprised cameriere. After a few inquiries, a few phone calls and a few twenties a sleepy unshaven man appeared with an unlit cigarette in his mouth and a massive ring of keys in his pocket. The gate to Arethusa's spring was unlocked and I walked down to the spring's edge.

The Greeks were wrong. I tasted the sacred water of Arethusa and can confirm it is not from the Peloponnese. That water is from Graham Creek in southern Indiana. I tasted the corn fields and hot summer nights and deer and oak trees and sunburns and laughing friends around a campfire on the Fourth of July. Arethusa is a Hoosier.

I made my offering to the nymph, thanked her yawning guardian and climbed out to turn my attention to the Mediterranean. Some of the fishing boats were beginning to come in, but not the little red one with the solitary hunched figure. He was still fishing, still searching.

I walked back to the café and ordered another coffee. I took the coffee and walked away. They did not call after me or even look where I was going. They knew I would pay. I walked up to the terrace above the nymphaeum to where a tall dark man in an apron was sweeping the pavement in front of a restaurant.

'Bongiorno,' I said, holding out the coffee.

'Bongiorno. Grazie.'

He leaned his broom against a table and accepted the coffee.

'Where do you get your fish?'

'From the local fishermen.'

'Like those boats out there?'

'Yes. They bring their catch in later in the morning.'

'I'm going to come back at noon and I want a fresh fish.'

'Yes.'

'But not any fresh fish,' I said. 'I want a fish from that boat right there. The red one.'

He squinted out at the boat and squinted back at me.

'I just watched him catch a fish and I'm going to eat it for lunch. When I come back at noon I'm going to sit down and you are going to bring me a fresh fish. That fish will be the one he just caught.'

He glanced down to the café, where I had been sitting with the locals and venerating the nymph. He looked at me and sipped his coffee and spoke.

'Certamente.'

'I want your best table. This one overlooking the sea. Don't open the awning because I want to sit in the sun. Keep it for me.'

'Si, naturalmente. How many will be in your party?'

'One.'

It was the best fish I ever ate.

www.ingramcontent.com/pod-product-compliance
Lightning Source LLC
LaVergne TN
LVHW091141080826
845145LV00008B/2217

* 9 7 8 1 9 4 9 2 6 7 5 6 3 *